649713

P9-ASN-575

DATE DUE

Demco, Inc. 38-293

To Richard

The Octette Bridge Club

A PLAY

by P.J. Barry

LITTLE COUNTRY THEATRE

SAMUEL FRENCH, INC.

45 WEST 25TH STREET   NEW YORK 10010
7623 SUNSET BOULEVARD   HOLLYWOOD 90046
LONDON   *TORONTO*

THE MUSIC BOX

IRVING BERLIN AND THE SHUBERT ORGANIZATION, OWNERS

KENNETH WAISSMAN   LOU KRAMER

in association with
M.T.M. ENTERPRISES, INC.

present

(in alphabetical order)

GISELA CALDWELL	**BETTE HENRITZE**
PEGGY CASS	**ELIZABETH HUDDLE**
LOIS de BANZIE	**NANCY MARCHAND**
ELIZABETH FRANZ	**ANNE PITONIAK**

in

THE OCTETTE BRIDGE CLUB

A new play by
P. J. BARRY

Scenery designed by	Costumes designed by	Lighting designed by
JOHN LEE BEATTY	**CARRIE ROBBINS**	**ROGER MORGAN**

General Management	Press Representatives	Casting	Production Stage Manager
THEATRE NOW, INC.	**HUNT/PUCCI ASSOCIATES**	**JOHNSON/LIFF ASSOCIATES**	**STEVE BECKLER**

Directed by
TOM MOORE

Professional premiere at Actors Theatre of Louisville

The Producers and Theatre Management are Members
of The League of New York Theatres and Producers, Inc.

Martha (Mrs. Michael McDermitt) . . . . ANNE PITONIAK

Mary (Margaret Donavan) . . . . BETTE HENRITZE

Connie (Mrs. David Emerson) . . . . NANCY MARCHAND

Nora (Mrs. Lawrence Hiller) . . . . ELIZABETH FRANZ

Alice (Mrs. Walter Monahan) . . . . LOIS de BANZIE

Ann (Mrs. John Conroy) . . . . ELIZABETH HUDDLE

Lil (Mrs. Peter Carmody) . . . . PEGGY CASS

Betsy (Mrs. Daniel Bailey) . . . . GISELA CALDWELL
and

Robert Foster, the photographer . . . . NICHOLAS KALEDIN

The action takes place in the living room of Ann (Mrs. John Conroy) in a Rhode Island town.

ACT I
A Friday night in late October, 1934.

ACT II
The night before Halloween, 1944.

THE OCTETTE BRIDGE CLUB was given its professional premiere at The Actors Theatre of Louisville.

In the cast were:

MARTHA (Mrs. Michael McDermott).....Sylvia Gassell
MARY (Margaret Donavan)..........Elizabeth Moore
CONNIE (Mrs. David Emerson).......Gloria Cromwell
NORA (Mrs. Lawrence Hiller).........Ruth Livingston
ALICE (Mrs. Walter Monahan) ....Sally Parrish
ANN (Mrs. John Conroy) ....Lynn Cohen
LIL (Mrs. Peter Carmody) ....Mary Shelley
BETSY (Mrs. Daniel Bailey)...............Beth Dixon
ROBERT FOSTER, the Photographer .....John Huffman

Directed by Robert Spera
Scenery designed by Paul Owen
Costumes designed by Marcia Dixcy
Lighting designed by Geoffrey T. Cunningham
Movement Coach, Rebecca Nixon
Stage Manager, Richard Cunningham
Assistant Stage Manager, Janice Neustedter

THE OCTETTE BRIDGE CLUB was first read as part of the first stage program at Center Stage, Baltimore, Maryland.

THE CAST

The eight sisters (In order of birth:)

	Act One 1934 Age	*Act Two* 1944 Age
MARTHA (Mrs. Michael McDermitt)	54	64
MARY (Margaret Donavan)	51	61
NORA (Mrs. Lawrence Hiller)	48	58
CONNIE (Mrs. David Emerson)	46	56
ALICE (Mrs. Walter Monahan)	44	54
ANN (Mrs. John Conroy)	43	53
LIL (Mrs. Peter Carmody)	40	50
BETSY (Mrs. Daniel Bailey)	37	47
ROBERT FOSTER (Photographer)	27	

*NOTES

Martha wears glasses. Nora and Alice use glasses to play cards.

In Act Two Martha, Nora and Alice wear glasses throughout.

In Act One, Scene 2, Nora accompanies Lil when she sings. However, any one of the sisters could be this piano player if a casting problem arises. Lil, of course, should play piano.

MUSIC

Before the play begins and between the scenes piano music *only* is suggested.

The action of the play takes place in the living room of Ann (Mrs. John Conroy) in a town in Rhode Island.

ACT ONE — A Friday night in late October, 1934.

ACT TWO — The Friday night before Halloween, October, 1944.

THE SETTING:

A middle class living room. Upstage left is an archway which leads into the front foyer and the hallway. Upstage right leads into a dining room (partially visible) and the kitchen (unseen).

In this living room along with wall accessories (two landscapes, knick-knack shelf, etc.) are the following: a fireplace, a small couch, two matching easy chairs, a console radio, an upright piano, and on the floor, a Persian rug. The furnishings are in keeping with the fashion of the time.

In both acts the matching chairs are moved about to make way for two card tables and eight chairs. The eight chairs are four straight backed dining room chairs, and four wooden folding chairs. In the 1st act there are two small jack-o-lanterns on top of the piano.

The above applies to Act One. In Act Two (ten years later) there are changes . . . slip covers for the chairs, a new console radio, a new lamp.

8

The Octette Bridge Club

ACT ONE

Scene 1

Place: *The living room in the home of ANN (Mrs. John Conroy) in a Rhode Island town.*

Time: *A Friday night in late October, 1934. At two card tables sit eight sisters, the Octette Bridge Club. They range in age from thirty-seven to fifty-four. At the card table right sitting clockwise: BETSY, NORA, CONNIE and MARY. At the card table left sitting clockwise: ANN, LIL, MARTHA and ALICE. They are, obviously, posing for a picture. At table left ALICE is the dummy, at table right MARY is the dummy. The OTHERS each hold a hand of cards. Each woman is conservatively dressed, and their hairdos are mostly of the marcelled fashion of the time. Downstage stands ROBERT FOSTER, a good looking young man of twenty seven. Beside him is a camera with a flash-bulb attachment set on a wooden tripod. Beside him on the floor there is a tin carrying case, and portable equipment.*

FOSTER. Hold it! (*They preen, all sitting very erect, with serious expressions. He takes the picture. They relax a little, relieved, a shifting about, a few giggles, etc.*)

BETSY. (*rising*) I'm the youngest of the eight sisters, Mr. Foster. I may not look it but I am.

MARTHA. (*rising*) I am the oldest. I claim that distinctive spot . . . and I certainly look it.

CONNIE. You certainly do.

MARY. Connie.

ALICE. Connie is the cut-up of the family.

MARY. She always was.

CONNIE. Always will be.

ANN. We should be quiet. Let Mr. Foster take our picture for the Providence Journal and then we can play bridge.

FOSTER. We're doing just fine.

LIL. Don't mind us, Mr. Foster, we get like a bunch of school girls when we're together. (*They giggle again.*)

FOSTER. All right . . . Yes, hold your cards . . . yes. (*Once more they sit up, very erect.*) Ready. Good. Ready . . . Hold it! (*He takes another picture. They again relax, chatter, their laughter increases, etc.*) Now let's see if I remember. (*And he makes use of a small notebook.*) You're the youngest . . . Mrs. Bailey.

BETSY. Yes.

FOSTER. And you're the oldest . . . Mrs. McDermitt.

MARTHA. Yes. I was the firstborn.

MARY. Second.

NORA. Third.

CONNIE. Fourth. Exactly eight pounds.

ALICE. Fifth.

ANN. Sixth.

LIL. Seventh.

BETSY. Eighth. We were all born before the turn of the century.

CONNIE. You don't have to give him that information.

BETSY. And if I hadn't been born there never would've been any Octette Bridge Club.

MARTHA. (*rising*) Our parents were Mr. and Mrs. Frank Donavan. (*sits*)

ALICE. Of Irish descent.

MARY. Catholics, of course.

MARTHA. God rest their souls.

OTHERS. God rest their souls.

FOSTER. Fine. Now, let's see if I have some of the facts straight about your children.

BETSY. Well, I have two children, a girl and a boy.

LIL. Me, too. A girl and a boy.

FOSTER. Little Lil and Little Peter.

LIL. That's right. Little Lil and Little Peter. Isn't he smart.

FOSTER. (*moving about the room*) You have two boys, Mrs. Hiller.

NORA. Yes, I do. Lawrence Junior and Thomas.

FOSTER. And you have three children, Mrs. Monahan?

ALICE. Oh, no, no. My husband and I don't have any children. But since our parents passed away, my sister Mary lives with us and she's . . . our big child.

MARY. Oh, Alice.

MARTHA. Now let's get back on the track so we don't get Mr. Foster confused. Ann.

ANN. I have the three children, Theodore, Elizabeth and James. But their nicknames are Teddy, Betty and Jimmy.

MARTHA. Connie.

CONNIE. I have four boys, three cats, two canaries and a snake. Have you got that Mr. Foster?

FOSTER. I think so, Mrs. Emerson.

MARTHA. I have four daughters. Joan, Jean, Jeannette and Janice. My husband and I were partial to J's.

CONNIE. Obviously. (*OTHERS giggle.*)

BETSY. (*rising*) Excuse me. I forgot to tell you, I'm sorry. My children's names are Kathleen and Daniel, Junior.

FOSTER. Oh.

BETSY. I'm sorry.

FOSTER. It's okay.

BETSY. I really am.

FOSTER. It's nothing to worry about.

MARTHA. Off the track again, Mr. Foster?

FOSTER. Not yet, Mrs. McDermitt. I know that you are the Principal of Clayton Junior High . . . in Cranston.

MARTHA. Absolutely correct.

FOSTER. And your husband is the lawyer?

MARTHA. No, no, my husband is deceased. I am a widow.

ALICE. Connie's husband is the lawyer.

CONNIE. (*rises*) The firm of Emerson, Frazer, Masters and Muldoon in Providence. And I am the only of us who married a Protestant. (*sits*)

ANN. My husband, as you know, Mr. Foster, is Sheriff Conroy.

BETSY. My husband, Dan, is a salesman. All over Rhode Island.

ALICE. My husband *owns* Wally's Variety Store at 99 Woodside Street.

LIL. (*rises*) My husband is an electrical engineer and he is shorter than I am and it has never bothered either of us. (*sits*)

FOSTER. And what does your husband do, Mrs. Hiller?

NORA. My husband, Larry, is a night watchman for Eckhart Mills. I love him very much.

MARY. Isn't that nice.

FOSTER. (*to MARY*) And your husband is . . .

MARY. (*rises*) I'm the only sister who is unmarried. I am Mary Margaret Donavan. I'm a bookkeeper for the Eastern Water Company in Jericho. As Alice said, I live with her and her husband Wally . . . my kind brother-in-law. (*sits*)

ALICE. Who owns Wally's Variety Store at 99 Woodside Street.

CONNIE. Lil, who does Mr. Foster remind you of?

LIL. Who?

CONNIE. Doesn't he look like Buddy Johnson.

LIL. (*rises*) Oh! Oh, you do! Oh, he does. Oh, Mr. Foster!

CONNIE. We both loved Buddy Johnson.

LIL. Oh, we did. He was so handsome. Dumb, but handsome. (*sits*)

FOSTER. Thank you very much, Mrs. Carmody.

LIL. Oh, no offense, Mr. Foster.

ANN. Can we drop the subject.

MARTHA. Yes, please.

MARY. What ever happened to Buddy Johnson?

ALICE. He drank himself to death.

MARTHA. God rest his soul.

OTHERS. God rest his soul.

ALICE. Just like his father and his father before him.

LIL. If you want any details about anything, Mr. Foster, you just ask our Alice.

MARTHA. Lil, let Mr. Foster get back on the track.

LIL. All abooooard!

CONNIE. (*whistle sound*) Woo! Woo! (*They all giggle.*)

FOSTER. Now let's see . . . when did you start the Octette Bridge Club?

ALICE. Three years ago.

MARTHA. This is our third anniversary.

LIL. So tonight is a very special occasion.

MARY. And it's been so nice since we started. Nothing could make me happier. All of us get together every other Friday—

ALICE. Twice a month.

MARY. It's always joyous.

MARTHA. It has been grand.

FOSTER. And how did it come about? Whose idea was it?

MARTHA. All of us.

NORA. No, no. It was Ann. It started right here in her house.

BETSY. I didn't even know how to play.

ANN. Actually it was Lil's idea . . . I simply got it organized.

LIL. Credit where credit is due. Ann got it off the ground, she did.

ANN. And I persuaded Betsy and Nora and Connie to learn how to play—

LIL. Betsy was the slowest.

CONNIE. And now we're three of the best players.

NORA. Yes, we are. (*BETSY rises, moves away from the table.*)

FOSTER. And you meet twice a month?

ANN. Yes.

ALICE. It gives us the opportunity to get together, to share. As children we always had one another . . . we were always a close knit family.

ANN. And, of course, we have some rules.

FOSTER. Like what?

CONNIE. Oh, boy.

ANN. Always pick your sister for a bridge partner. (*They laugh.*)

LIL. Don't take your bridge game too seriously.

ALICE. And don't argue before, during—

MARY. —Or after a game.

MARTHA. And never once, Mr. Foster, has the smallest argument occurred.

CONNIE. May God forgive you, Martha.

ANN. And wherever the bridge games takes place—we rotate from house to house—refreshments and beverages are always served by the hostess after the card playing is completed for the evening.

FOSTER. Alcoholic beverages?

ANN. Oh, no. No. None of us indulge . . . in that.

FOSTER. None of you?

MARTHA. (*rising*) Of course not. Our father was head of the Temperence League. And none of us smoke cigarettes either.

ANN. None of us.

MARTHA. Isn't that remarkable in 1934? (*sits*)

CONNIE. We may not drink or smoke but, believe me, there is not a saint among us.

ANN. Connie, speak for yourself.

CONNIE. Are you married, Mr. Foster?

·MARTHA. Will you behave.

FOSTER. I'm engaged, Mrs. Emerson. (*A chorus of disappointment. He laughs, returning to his camera.*) All right now, would you pick up the cards again, please.

LIL. Here we go!

ALICE. Is this the last   NORA. Betsy
picture that you're taking?

FOSTER. Yes, it is, Mrs. Monahan. (*They express their*

displeasure.) Hold it, please. Ready. Mrs. Bailey? (*pause*) Mrs. Bailey?

NORA. Betsy.

BETSY. What? Oh, I'm sorry. (*crosses to her place at the table and sits*)

FOSTER. The cards.

BETSY. I'm sorry. (*picks up hand of cards*)

LIL. She's our daydreamer.

FOSTER. Thank you.

BETSY. You're welcome.

FOSTER. Hold it, everyone. Ready. . . ! (*He takes the picture. Again, they chatter, a few giggles, etc.*)

CONNIE. Thank God.

MARTHA. Connie.

CONNIE. I'm the most religious, Mr. Foster. I'm sure you noticed.

LIL. She is not.

CONNIE. Mr. Foster is aware that I am the most religious. You are aware, Mr. Foster.

FOSTER. (*going along with her*) Yes, I am, Mrs. Emerson.

LIL. Well, she isn't. Mary is.

CONNIE. That is true. All right, I'll concede. Mary was going to become a nun . . . but she couldn't get into the habit. (*She gets a few groans.*)

ANN. May I offer you some refreshments before you leave?

FOSTER. No, thank you. I have to be getting along. (*They express their displeasure.*) I've enjoyed meeting all of you. (*A chorus of response.*) And thank you very much. (*A chorus of appreciation.*)

LIL. (*rising, following him*) We all love the *Providence Journal.*

ANN. I'll show you out. (*putting on a sweater*)

LIL. (*following him to archway*) It will be in the Rotogravure section a week from Sunday?

FOSTER. Yes, it will, Mrs. Carmody.

ALICE. We can't wait. We'll be the talk of the town.

CONNIE. Don't count on it. Let's hear it for Mr. Foster.

ALL. Rah! Rah! Rah!

FOSTER. Bye, now. (*Goodbyes are repeated. FOSTER exits with ANN.*)

LIL. (*calling after him*) Have a happy Halloween!

CONNIE. (*chuckles*) Have a happy Halloween!

LIL. What's wrong with that? I hope he does.

(*And through the following LIL takes the two small candy-filled jack-o-lanterns from atop the piano. She helps herself to a candy, then sets a jack-o-lantern at each card table. CONNIE goes and gets card sets and scoring pads and sets them at each table, and she sits again. All of them, almost immediately on their feet, begin adjusting corsets, bra straps and stockings. Some of them make use of their purses.*)

NORA. Very likable, wasn't he.

MARY. Oh, yes, wasn't he a nice boy.

ALICE. Oh, very nice.

BETSY. I'll bet he thought we were cuckoo.

NORA. No, he didn't.

LIL. We were just acting a little silly.

CONNIE. Not me.

MARTHA. You were the worst. Your behavior was outrageous.

CONNIE. He thought I was charming.

LIL. Oh, won't it be a thrill to see our picture in the Rotogravure. We'll be as famous as Jean Harlow!

MARTHA. Listen to her.   CONNIE. Easy, Lil,
Tsk, tsk, tsk.   easy.

NORA. Are you all right, Betsy?

BETSY. I'm fine, Nora.

NORA. You looked like you were going to cry before
. . . when Mr. Foster was about to take that last picture.

LIL. Betsy always looks like she's going to cry. .

BETSY. I do not. I just don't think it's necessary to try
and smile all the time.

LIL. Who tries? I don't try. It comes naturally.

MARTHA. Laugh and the world laughs with you, cry
and you cry alone.

ALICE and MARY. (*overlapping*) —cry alone.

MARTHA. Self pity never did anyone any good. It's to
be avoided. (*LIL goes into the dining room and soon returns with a plate of cookies. She eats one.*)

BETSY. Who said anything about self pity? No one
said—

MARTHA. Someone just said something about it or
something similar to it.

BETSY. Who?

MARTHA. It doesn't matter. Self-pity is self-pity, and
that's all there is to it.

BETSY. No one said *anything* about—

MARTHA. Are you accusing me of a fabrication?

CONNIE. Are you calling Martha a liar?

NORA. Martha, she's not calling you a liar.

MARY. Martha's right, somebody did say something
about self-pity, didn't they—

ALICE. (*overlapping*) Exactly. Cry and you cry alone.

LIL. Somebody's a liar. Not me. Who? (*looks at
BETSY*)

MARTHA. Betsy has the answer to that question.

NORA. Or somebody.

MARTHA. But we'll overlook it because this is our third anniversary, a night of celebration, not a night for dissension.

MARY. True.   ALICE. Exactly.

(*And through the following MARTHA begins to stretch a little, doing very restrained exercises. She is soon joined by ALICE and MARY. BETSY joins them for a bit.*)

MARTHA. Before Ann gets back let's stretch, girls.

LIL. (*having wandered to the piano, plays a few chords*) Ann's had the piano tuned. Such a nice sound. I wonder who tuned it?

ALICE and MARY. Joe Coughlin.

LIL. Is he still tuning?

ALICE and MARY. Oh, yes.

MARTHA. I thought he was dead.

ALICE and MARY. Oh, no.

MARTHA. I'm so surprised. I didn't know he was still alive, let alone still tuning.

ALICE and MARY. Oh, yes.

NORA. Such a nice man.

ALICE. Too bad about his boys though.

MARY. (*emphatically*) Oh, yes. Yes, yes, it is!

LIL. What about his boys?

ALICE. Well, Joe Junior went to New York and became a stickup man and now he's in jail.

LIL. Oh, no.

ALICE and MARY. Oh, yes.

MARY. True.   MARTHA.   LIL. So sad.
                Tsk, tsk, tsk.

ALICE. And his second son, George, a saxophone player got into—correct me if I'm wrong, Mary—dope addiction and wound up with a damaged brain in one of those places and not even thirty years old.

BETSY. One of those places what?

MARY. Joe's son is at the state institution.

ALICE. True.

MARY. Exactly.   MARTHA. Tsk, tsk, tsk.

MARTHA. What ever happened to that shameless woman he married?

MARY. No one knows.

NORA. I liked her.

MARTHA. Really, Nora.

NORA. Well, I did.

ALICE. She deserted them when the boys were still in knickers.

MARY. Just ran off with another man, a piano player.

MARTHA. (*pause*) A piano player?!

ALICE. Oh, yes.

MARY. (*overlapping*) True.

MARTHA. Oh, the irony.

LIL. The man she ran off with was a piano player?

ALICE and MARY. Oh, yes.

ALICE. Veronica Coughlin ran off with a piano player.

MARTHA. The irony, the irony!

CONNIE. Joe wasn't tuning her keys properly so she wanted someone who would.

BETSY. (*laughing*) Oh,   NORA. (*returning to
Connie . . . (*sits*)   her bridge chair*) Oh,
                                     Connie.

MARTHA. Connie, you are so sassy, so bold. (*sits*)

CONNIE. Sometimes a little devil—hardly visible— jumps into my mouth and pokes at my tongue with his tiny pitchfork. (*begins to deal*)

LIL. I can never understand a woman deserting her own children, her own flesh and blood. Why? (*sits*)

CONNIE. I just told you why. L-u-s-t.

MARY. Oh, Connie. (*Returns to her bridge chair; ALICE returns to her chair, soon deals.*)

BETSY. Lust.

MARTHA. There's no need to talk like that.

BETSY. I didn't say it, Connie did.

MARTHA. Connie didn't say it, she spelled it out.

BETSY. Lust.

MARTHA. Why are you repeating that word?

BETSY. (*pause*) I don't know.

ALICE. (*as ANN returns*) Mr. Foster seemed to enjoy himself, didn't he.

ANN. Wait 'til you hear!

LIL. I just hope that we didn't break the camera. (*laughter*)

ANN. Do you know where the *Providence Journal* is sending that boy next week?

LIL. Where?

ANN. To Callandar, Canada! To photograph the Dionne Quintuplets! (*a burst of wild enthusiasm*)

ALICE. Oh! Oh! Oh!   NORA. Oh, my!

MARY. Oh, isn't that nice!

ALICE. Oh, yes!

ANN. (*overlapping*) Isn't that exciting?

MARTHA. (*overlapping*) Oh, isn't that exciting!

LIL. Oh, I wish I were going with him. I'd love to see all those tiny, tiny babies . . . isn't he lucky?

ANN. I seemed more excited about it than he did.

LIL. The boy who photographed us will be photographing the Dionne Quintuplets!

BETSY. I hope they don't die before he gets there. (*Silence. Most of them turn to her in disbelief.*)

ANN. The Quintuplets will not die.

MARY. Doctor DaFoe will not let them.

ALICE. Betsy, don't be so gloomy.

LIL. Look on the bright side.

BETSY. They're fragile. It could happen.

ALICE. It won't

ANN. Don't say things like that.

NORA. These cards are so colorful, aren't they, Betsy?

BETSY. Yes, they are.

CONNIE. Can we get this game on the road?

LIL. (*rising*) Not 'til I get back.

CONNIE. What?

LIL. I'm thirsty. (*crosses into dining room, exits into kitchen*)

ALICE. Not again.

ANN. Well, we'll have to wait. Both tables must start at the same time.

CONNIE. (*crossing to dining room*) Oh, Ann, you and your dumb rules.

NORA. Where did you get these cards, Ann?

ANN. In Jericho. At La Massney's.

CONNIE. (*shouting off*) Lil, get the heck back in here so we can start this darn game!

NORA. (*overlapping*) La Massney's is a nice store. I like to shop there.

ANN. They have most everything you need in the stationary and card line.

ALICE. Was *Nannette La Massney* there?

ANN. Yes, she was. She was on the cash register.

MARTHA. Who is Nannette La Massney?

ALICE. You know, Martha. She's the one who was *sent away* for awhile.

BETSY. When I go in La Massney's she's very . . . confidential with me.

CONNIE. Uh huh.

ALICE. She was put away some time back because she *punched* her mother in the face until she *broke* her mother's nose.

MARY. Isn't that ter-   MARTHA. Tsk, tsk, tsk.
rible.

ALICE. She was sent to the state institution . . . like
Joe Coughlin's son.

MARY. No, Alice, not so. Forgive me for correcting
you, but her husband, Roland La Massney, put her in
that special place in Woonsocket.

ALICE. Quidnekka Hall, Mary.

MARY. Quidnekka Hall. You're right, Alice.

ANN. (*having moved to dining room area*) Lil, don't
you touch that cake! (*some responsive laughter*)

BETSY. (*overlapping*) Nannette La Massney scares
me. Her eyes.

CONNIE. She recognizes one of her own.

BETSY. You mean that I'm cuckoo, too? Is that what
you're saying?

CONNIE. I'm only teasing.

BETSY. I only get . . . melancholy now and then. I'm
not cuckoo. (*moves away from the card table*)

CONNIE. Betsy, I was teasing.

ANN. You don't get melancholy, you get overtired.
You work too hard, that's all . . . the way you keep your
house . . . so spic and span.

BETSY. I'm not like Nannette La Massney.

NORA. She's fine now, Betsy.

BETSY. I'm not.

MARTHA. For heaven's sake, who said you were?

MARY. (*overlapping*) I'm glad Nannette is better. But
maybe she had good reason to go off the deep end when
she did.

MARTHA. What does that mean?

ALICE. It means — correct me, if I'm wrong, Mary —
that Nannette's husband Roland always had a cornucopia of lady friends. And he was never very discreet
about it.

BETSY. So the real reason Nannette La Massney went cuckoo was because her husband was unfaithful to her?

ALICE. I believe that has a lot to do with it. Wouldn't you say, Mary?

MARY. (*emphatically*) Oh, yes, definitely, Alice, oh, yes!

CONNIE. S-e-x takes the blame for so much.

BETSY. It's not her fault if her husband strayed.

MARTHA. Did anyone say it was her fault? I don't think any of us said that, I don't think any of us would, would we?

NORA. Can we talk about something else?

ANN. I think it's time to drop the subject, girls.

MARTHA. I second the motion. All in favor? (*raises hand*)

OTHERS. (*raising hands*) I.

MARTHA. All opposed?

CONNIE. (*raising hand*) I.

MARTHA. Connie, you are outnumbered.

ANN. Subject dropped. Nannette La Massney's had enough trouble without us gossiping about—

BETSY. I'm not like Nannette La Massney.

MARTHA. Are you starting that again.

BETSY. I'm not. (*rushes out into the hall, exits*)

ANN. Betsy! (*moves into the hallway after her*)

LIL. (*returning from kitchen with a glass of soda*) Oh, I'd give my right arm to see all those tiny, tiny babies. What's the matter?

ANN. Betsy. She's in the bathroom.

ALICE. She certainly is moody tonight.

MARY. Oh, yes.

MARTHA. I always find myself saying the wrong thing to her.

ANN. She's very upset.

ALICE. *Very* upset?

MARY. Ann says so.

MARTHA. Why?

LIL. Don't look at me. I don't know.

NORA. She's upset about Nannette La Massney.

CONNIE. (*having moved to the hallway*) Betsy, hurry up! Your smart partner's got a beautiful hand!

ANN. I'm afraid she's upset about Dan.

MARY. What about Dan?

CONNIE. Hell will freeze over before we start this darn game.

MARTHA. Watch your language.

ALICE. What about Dan?

ANN. He's too handsome for his own good.

LIL. What does that mean?

ANN. It means Dan is—

CONNIE. Well, here you are. (*BETSY returns.*)

NORA. Are you feeling better, Betsy?

ANN. I think she is.

MARY. I hope so, Betsy.

CONNIE. Now you sit down, you silly goose, so we can start this darn game. (*as LIL rises*) Lil, you are not going back to that kitchen. Sit down.

LIL. I touched nothing. (*She sits. They all laugh. Now all are seated again. Cards have been dealt.*)

BETSY. I'm sorry. I don't know what's gotten into me tonight.

MARTHA. We're sorry, too, Betsy. We didn't mean to upset you.

BETSY. I guess it's all the excitement about our photographs.

ANN. Of course.

LIL. We're all excited, too, Betsy. Just think! We'll soon be more famous than the Dionne Quintuplets!

CONNIE. I open with one heart. Finally.

LIL. You know those five babies were so tiny when they were born that you could hold one in the palm of your hand, in the—

MARY. One spade.

LIL. —palm of your hand. (*illustrates*) A miracle that the five of them survived.

MARTHA. God bless them.

ALL. God bless them.

BETSY. Did you know that the Chicago Exposition wanted the quintuplets for an exhibition . . . but Dr. DaFoe wouldn't permit it.

ANN. Of course not.

BETSY. And do you know what the hit of the Chicago Exposition *is*? That strip tease lady, Sally Rand.

ALICE. One diamond.

BETSY. She uses feathers and fans.

LIL. Did you ever hear such a thing?!

MARTHA. Who told you that trash?

BETSY. Dan.

MARTHA. Of course.

BETSY. It's not trash, it's facts.

MARTHA. Tsk, tsk, tsk.

NORA. Betsy, it's your bid.

BETSY. Oh. Two hearts.

ANN. Pass.

LIL. Won't it be a treat a week from Sunday to buy the paper and see all of us? The Third Anniversary of the Octette Bridge Club! I can't wait.

ALICE. It would make Mama happy.

MARY. Poppa, too.

LIL. (*sings an old childhood song, and each of them finally joins in*)

"Old Dog Tray, ever faithful
Grief shall not drive him away
He is gentle, he is kind
No better friend you'll find
No better friend than Old Dog Tray."
(*silence*)

NORA. Pass. (*silence*)

LIL. One spade.

MARTHA. Pass. (*silence*)

CONNIE. I wonder if Mr. Foster guessed how many of us have false teeth? (*They all roar.*)

Blackout

SCENE 2

*It is approximately two hours later. The card games are
    completed, refreshments have been served. A few
    glasses, one cup and saucer and a plate with cookies
    remain.*

*During the blackout we hear an introduction to a popu-
    lar love song of yesteryear. At rise of lights LIL be-
    gins to sing the song with dramatic intensity. NORA
    accompanies her at the piano. BETSY, though lis-
    tening, is seated by herself at a card table playing
    solitaire. In the middle of the song BETSY loudly
    joins in with LIL until she is hushed by CONNIE.
    LIL finishes the song to a good round of applause.*

ALICE. Lil, you should've gone on the stage.

LIL. I know. But Mama and Poppa didn't approve.

NORA. I love hearing you sing, Lil. I'll never forget
the first time you sang in the choir.

LIL. Singing in the choir is still one of the joys of my life. It makes you feel closer to God.

MARTHA. Oh, yes.

LIL. (*finishing some cake*) But isn't it funny? Little Lillian can hardly carry a tune.

ANN. That's the way it is. I can hardly carry a tune . . . but my Betty sings like a bird.

MARTHA. Oh, she does.

CONNIE. She gets that from her father.

ANN. I suppose I have to face that.

NORA. Well, you may not sing like a bird but your devil's food cake was delicious.

CONNIE. Wasn't it.   LIL. Mmm, yummy.

ALICE. What's the matter, Mary?

MARY. Nothing. (*sits down*)

ALICE. Are you having that feeling again? (*MARY nods, breathless.*)

MARTHA. Mary, what is it?

ANN. I'll get some water. (*She quickly exits. OTHERS gather around MARY. BETSY rises, remains nearby.*)

ALICE. She felt it this morning just after she had her grapefruit juice. Wally and I both thought that she should go and see Dr. Carroll . . . but she wouldn't hear of it.

MARY. It's going away.

NORA. Do you want me to call Dr. Carroll now?

MARY. No. It's going away. Just a little dizziness. And something I ate last night, I'm sure.

ALICE. We went to Providence last night. We went to Ming Chow's for dinner. She had egg roll . . . to start.

MARTHA. Oh, Mary, you didn't have egg roll.

MARY. I know, I know, it never agrees with me. But sometimes I can't resist. I'm sure it's the egg roll.

MARTHA. Of course it's the egg roll. You should know better.

MARY. I know, I know.

ANN. (*returning with a glass of water*) Here, Mary. Drink this.

MARTHA. Oh, Mary-Mary-Mary . . . egg roll.

MARY. I know, I know.

ALICE. I warned her.

MARTHA. (*nodding*) The egg roll *and* the grapefruit combination.

NORA. Will you get a complete examination soon? Will you do that for yourself?

MARY. I will, Nora. Soon.

LIL. Doctor Carroll said I should get more exercise.

ALICE. We all should.

BETSY. I walk a lot.

MARY. (*to ALICE*) The egg roll . . .

ALICE & MARY & MARTHA. . . . and the grapefruit juice. (*And the three nod in unison.*)

BETSY. I walk everywhere. I think nothing of walking to Jericho and back.

MARY. A good night's sleep will do the trick.

ALICE. Of course it will.

BETSY. Dan says it's good for me.

ALICE. The combination of the lack of sleep—

MARY. And the egg roll—

MARTHA. *And* the grapefruit juice.

BETSY. Dan says walking is good for my figure.

ALICE. True.   MARTHA. Of course.

MARY. I know, I know.

BETSY. Dan and I used to walk everywhere together.

ANN. Mary, can I get you a cup of tea?

MARY. No, thanks, dear. I'm fine, really. The water is sufficient.

BETSY. Maybe you should do more walking, Mary. You could walk with me to Jericho. We could walk together.

ALICE. Not now, Betsy.

MARTHA. (*rising*) I'm just tired. It's time to go home anyway, isn't it?

ALICE. According to my new Bulova, it's two minutes to eleven.

NORA. Oh! Larry will be home early tonight. (*Everyone begins to collect their things.*)

MARY. Let's go home now, Alice.

ALICE. Certainly, Mary. We'll have you home in jig time and you can get a good night's sleep.

BETSY. Dan and I used to go for long walks in the woods. Why don't we do that anymore.

MARTHA. Because you have two children to tend to, silly.

BETSY. I'm a good mother.

MARTHA. Of course you are. Well, it is about that time to wend our way homeward.

LIL. Uh huh. Party's over. Back to reality, girls.

(*MARTHA, MARY, LIL & ALICE are moving out of the room into the hallway. ANN has followed. Through the following we can hear the muffled voices from the hallway where they are getting into coats and hats.*)

NORA. Mary does look pale: and she's lost weight.

BETSY. You think there's something really wrong with her?

CONNIE. It's probably just that time for her.

BETSY. What time?

CONNIE. The change.

BETSY. The change?

NORA. The change of life.

BETSY. Oh. (*pause*) And that gives you indigestion? I thought it was hot flashes.

NORA. Well, we'll know better after she sees Dr. Carroll. There's no need to worry about it now.

CONNIE. Oh, Nora, you're always so sensible.

NORA. We get enough to worry about without inviting it.

BETSY. Maybe I should see Dr. Carroll, too.

NORA. Why?

BETSY. I haven't been sleeping well lately.

CONNIE. Count pigs. That's what I do.

BETSY. Pigs? I thought it was sheep.

CONNIE. No, pigs . . . jumping over a fence (*With her hand she illustrates the jumping, and makes three pig snorts and then snoozes off. BETSY and NORA laugh. LIL moves back into the room followed by MARTHA, MARY and ALICE. They are now in their hats and coats and carrying their purses. They all wear hats. ANN returns, too.*)

LIL. How do you like this hat, girls?

MARY. It's zippy.

LIL. Isn't it? I love the feather. Everyone says it suits me. (*gives NORA her hat and coat*) Don't I look wicked?

BETSY. Like Sally Rand.

LIL. What? Who?

BETSY. Feathers. Sally Rand. The Chicago Exposition. Dan.

LIL. Oh! Ohhhh. (*laughs*) Did you ever hear such a thing?! Now that is wicked. (*laughs again*)

ANN. Are you feeling all right now, Mary?

MARY. Oh, yes, fine. That glass of water was so re-freshing.

NORA. The night air will perk you up, too.

MARTHA. Remember now, Sunday is All Saint's Day and we're all going to the cemetery to pay our respects.

ANN. I planned to.

ALICE. So did I.

MARY. Oh, yes.

CONNIE. I think we're all going.

MARTHA. What time? In the afternoon would be best for me.

LIL. We don't *have* to go together. I may not be able—

MARTHA. Mama and Poppa would like it if we were all there together to pay our respects. You know how much they loved seeing us all together. "You don't need any other friends. Always remember that you have one another."

NORA. It is probably easier if we all go by ourselves.

MARTHA. Mama and Poppa would like us all there to-gether. All Saint's Day was their favorite holy day of ob-ligation and we—

NORA. I can only speak for myself. Larry and I have promised the boys a special trip to Benson's Animal Farm before it closes for the winter.

MARTHA. We always go together on All Saints Day. Tradition is tradition. I'm surprised at you.

NORA. I'll go after seven o'clock mass.

MARTHA. The rest of us can't go to seven o'clock mass on Sunday at your parish, I'm sure of that. We'd all have to get up at the crack of dawn. I certainly have a distance to drive, Lil has a distance to—

NORA. We've made the plans.

MARTHA. Then postpone them. Your boys won't mind if—

NORA. Yes, they would. Larry and I promised them . . . for Halloween. And Larry was able to borrow his brother's car so we could make this special trip.

BETSY. Dan and I would have trouble on Sunday—

MARTHA. Hush, Betsy. (*to NORA*) I would suggest that you change your plans, Nora. Benson's Animal Farm will not—

ANN. Mama and Poppa—

NORA. I'm sorry, but Larry and the boys come first, you know that. They're alive . . . and Mama and Poppa—

BETSY. —are dead.

NORA. Yes. They are.

MARTHA. Their spirit lives on . . . if we want it to live on.

NORA. I'm sure they'll forgive me.

MARTHA. I doubt that.

NORA. On Sunday I will visit Mama and Poppa's grave after seven o'clock mass and I'll bring them a bunch of violets.

MARY. They always loved violets.

ALICE. True.

MARTHA. I have never heard you talk this way. You, of all of us! I'm shocked!

MARY. Martha, it's all right. Nora is just—

MARTHA. No, it is not all right. This would make Mama and Poppa very, very sad. All Saints Day.

CONNIE. You're making such a fuss over—

MARTHA. If I want to make a fuss, I'll make a fuss, thank you.

BETSY. Well, you are making a fuss.

MARTHA. That is enough out of you. (*pause*) And don't give me that look. I don't like that look.

LIL. (*lightly*) Well . . .

MARTHA. Now. I will be at the cemetery at three on Sunday afternoon. How many will be there to join me? May I see a show of hands? (*There is hesitation, then ANN raises her hand, followed by ALICE and MARY. Then LIL. Then CONNIE.*) Betsy, dear? (*BETSY, reluctantly, raises her hand.*) You see, Nora? We'll all be there on All Saints Day. And if you're not with us, Mama and Poppa will be disappointed. (*pause*) I'll say no more. (*She exits into hallway. LIL, to ease the tension, has turned her hat around until the feather is flopping in front of her face.*)

LIL. (*a pinched nose sound*) Everyone says this feather suits me. (*She puts her coat on backwards. OTHERS howl with laughter. Tough sounding babe . . . turning NORA's hat around:*) Whatya lookin' at? Whatya laughin' at? Me? Huh? Me? I'm classy. I don't come from the wrong side of the tracks, oh, no, not me. I'm no Portugie La La—

ANN. Lil!

LIL. —or a French Canuck!

ANN & ALICE. Lil!

MARY. Or a Methodist!

ANN, NORA, ALICE, CONNIE. Mary!

LIL. I'm a classy Irish Catholic lady, I am. (*And she struts around a card table, ALICE, MARY and NORA parading after her, getting their coats and hats on backwards.*)

CONNIE. You're a strumpet. (*And she rushes off.*)

LIL. (*as ANN laughs and exits*) Oh, yeah? I'm good enough to sing in the church choir. (*And she hits a high note.*)

MARTHA. (*returning with hat and coat on backwards*) All right! (*They scream with delight, more so when CON-*

*NIE returns with her hat and coat on backwards. And
again they scream as ANN returns wearing her husband's
hat and overcoat on backwards. It is a fool's parade.*)

CONNIE. Hey, Clyde! (*hooking arms with ANN*)
Ain't you Clyde? Bonnie and Clyde!

ANN. Oh. Ohhhh!

CONNIE. (*overlapping*) Hands in the air, all of ya!

ANN. Yeah! Hands in the air! (*Laughing, they all begin to play the game, raising their hands in the air.*)
You, too, flatfoot.

MARY. Who, me?

LIL. (*overriding the laughter*) This is the way Mr.
Foster should've taken our picture for the Rotogravure!
(*And that sends them all into uproarious laughter,
especially LIL and CONNIE. Each of them collapses
into the nearest chair. BETSY rushes off into the hallway.*)

MARY. (*pause*) Oh, oh . . . I'm aching. (*pause*) Oh.
Oh, I feel so much better. I haven't laughed like that in a
good many moons. (*BETSY appears in the hallway
archway. She has her coat and hat on backwards. She
laughs. They all turn, surprised.*) Oh, Betsy . . . (*ANN
attempts to laugh. There is a light murmur of laughter
from the others.*)

MARTHA. Well, enough is enough. Let's get out of
here now . . . before we're raided by the police. (*She exits into the hallway. Quick goodnights and movement
into the hallway area, and a rather formal atmosphere
resumes almost as if their display of spontaneous wacki-
ness hadn't occurred. CONNIE, BETSY, LIL and
NORA remain. BETSY sets down her hat and coat on a
chair.*)

LIL. (*righting her coat and hat*) Listen! On next year's

anniversary before Halloween, we should all come in costumes and the best costume will win a special prize.

CONNIE. Oh, boy.

LIL. Isn't that a grand idea?

CONNIE. Grand.

LIL. Come on, Nora. (*sings, as she moves into hallway*) *"I'm the Halloween girl, I'm the Halloween pearl . . . "* (*Exits; NORA now starts after her.*)

MARTHA. (*returning*) Nora, tonight before I go to sleep I shall get down on my knees and pray for you. I shall say a special prayer to St. Jude, Advocate of the Impossible, and ask him to assist you in reversing your Sunday cemetery decision.

NORA. St. Jude and I have never gotten along.

MARTHA. (*miffed*) Well, St. Jude and I have and I will intervene for you. (*exits*)

CONNIE. (*pause*) You are a troublemaker.

NORA. (*lightly*) I am not. I am an innocent. (*Exits; BETSY begins to clear things from the card tables.*)

CONNIE. Do you want a ride home with me?

BETSY. No, thanks. I'll walk.

CONNIE. At this hour?

BETSY. It's only a little after eleven.

CONNIE. It's pitch black out there tonight.

BETSY. I like the dark.

CONNIE. So do witches. They're all out there . . . getting ready for Halloween.

BETSY. You don't really think I'm cuckoo like Nannette La Massney, do you?

CONNIE. Oh, honestly, you're nothing like Nannette La Massney. You're too sensitive.

BETSY. Then why did you say that?

CONNIE. That was hours ago. You know I don't mean

half the things I say . . . the devil with his little pitch-fork. I love you, you silly goose.

BETSY. You do? You love me? I love you, too.

CONNIE. Are you sure you don't want a ride home?

BETSY. No. I'll help Ann before I go.

ANN. (*returning*) Oh, Betsy, ride with Connie. (*brings BETSY her coat, hat and purse*) It's late to be walking home by yourself.

BETSY. I'll be fine. I can help you straighten up.

ANN. There's practically nothing left to do.

BETSY. I can help you put the card tables away. (*sets her coat, hat and purse down*) Go along, Connie.

CONNIE. (*to BETSY*) You're a silly goose . . . that's what you are.

ANN. You're the silly goose.

CONNIE. Go sit on a tack. 'Night.

ALICE. Goodnight.   BETSY. 'Night, Connie.

(*CONNIE does a little improv dance, and ANN and BETSY laugh. CONNIE exits. They both laugh again lightly and start to go about the work.*)

BETSY. These cards are so colorful. Maybe I'll go to La Massney's tomorrow and get a set just like them.

ANN. Well, if you do don't let Nannette La Massney confide in you anymore. You don't want people thinking "birds-of-a-feather" . . . do you?

BETSY. (*defensively*) She's pleasant.

ANN. She's tilted. Not that we weren't a little bit tilted ourselves tonight. Talk about simpletons. (*BETSY begins to fold a table.*) You don't have to do that.

BETSY. I said I'd help.

ANN. Well, I appreciate it, but you don't have to.

BETSY. Danny and Kathleen like to make houses with my card tables. They get an old blanket from the attic, and they cover them and get under. It's cute.

ANN. Teddy and Betty like to do that, too.

BETSY. Especially on rainy days.

ANN. Yes, especially.

BETSY. We used to do that. You did that with me.

ANN. Yes, but mostly with chairs. Card tables or the like were a luxury when we were children.

BETSY. I loved it when you did that with me. You were always my favorite sister. Am I your favorite sister?

ANN. I don't have a favorite sister, you know that.

BETSY. I do. You must. Who?

ANN. Let's drop the subject. (*moves card table into hallway*)

BETSY. I'll tell you a secret.

ANN. You're always full of secrets.

BETSY. Do you want to hear?

ANN. If you tell me it won't be a secret anymore.

BETSY. I had my fortune told.

ANN. Oh?

BETSY. Yes!

ANN. That's all superstitious nonsense, Betsy. It's frowned on by the Church. (*picks up other folded card table, puts it against hallway wall*)

BETSY. It's not a sin, for heaven's sake. No harm done. I didn't take it very seriously. (*folds a wooden chair*) This fortune teller has a tiny little hole in the wall right next to McShane's Barber Shop. I was just walking along, on my way to Jericho, minding my own business when I suddenly stopped—like someone had touched me—and I noticed the sign. *Madame Gambino—For-*

tune Teller. I don't know what got into me, but I went right in.

ANN. (*continuing to work*) How much did it cost?

BETSY. (*hesitates*) One dollar.

ANN. (*taken aback*) One dollar! We are in the midst of a depression, you know. I have to be careful not to squander a dollar . . . and I know you have to—

BETSY. (*revved up*) Anyway, Madame Gamino—

ANN. And don't tell that to Martha. You'll never hear the end of it.

BETSY. Anyway, Madame Gambino guessed that I had seven sisters and she said two were schoolteachers . . . you and Martha.

ANN. She named our names?

BETSY. No. She just said two were teachers. Isn't that remarkable? (*sits in one of the four straight-backed dining room chairs resting awkwardly in the middle of the room*) She knew I had two children, just like that . . . and she guessed Dan was a salesman. (*rapidly*) And she said . . . she said I must be very careful of a buxom, blonde woman with almond-shaped eyes who might bring trouble into my life. But she said to continue to pray for happiness, particularly to the Blessed Virgin Mary who is partial to blessing auburn-haired women—Oh, I'd never heard such a thing either, but I liked hearing it—and she said for me to tell my intimate feelings to those closest to me, especially my sisters. Didn't she say a lot?

ANN. She certainly did! Madame Gambino, indeed! "The blessed Virgin Mary is partial to blessing auburn-haired—" —What nerve! Next time, Betsy Donavan

Bailey, I'd think twice about squandering a dollar on a woman who isn't qualified to give advice to a . . . a chicken.

BETSY. It was fun.

ANN. It was a waste of a dollar. Well, it is getting late. Here. Take the jack-o-lanterns for Kathleen and Danny. I have extras for mine. Shall I get you a paper bag for them?

BETSY. (*rising, holding a jack-o-lantern in each hand*) Do you want me to go home?

ANN. Dan will be waiting up for you, won't he?

BETSY. Oh, no. No. (*sits*) He had two clients that he had to wine and dine tonight. He said he'd be late. Probably midnight . . . or later.

ANN. Who's watching the children?

BETSY. Mary Lou from next door.

ANN. Oh, yes, Mary Lou. Does she still stutter?

BETSY. Yes, but she's improving.

ANN. Oh, good. I am a little tired, Betsy.

BETSY. (*rises*) Do you think I'm pretty, Ann?

ANN. Of course you're pretty. (*BETSY bursts into tears.*) Oh, Betsy, what is it? Don't cry. Do you have a hankerchief? (*goes and gets BETSY's purse*)

BETSY. I don't have one. I did the wash yesterday but I didn't do the whites. Only the darks. (*takes a napkin from nearby*)

ANN. Don't use that. It's soiled.

BETSY. (*using it*) I don't care.

ANN. Oh, what is it? You've got yourself into such a state.

BETSY. I'm sorry.

ANN. Calm down. Calm down now.

BETSY. I've been so upset. I don't know how to talk about it.

ANN. Is it something very personal?

BETSY. Yes. Oh, yes.

ANN. Then perhaps you should talk to Sister Margaret Theresa.

BETSY. Sister Margaret Theresa? Why would I. . . ? She's a nun.

ANN. Sister Margaret Theresa is very knowledgeable about—

BETSY. Sister Margaret Theresa knows nothing about *this*.

ANN. Sister Margaret Theresa was so helpful to Mama when she was in the hospital and always—

BETSY. Sister Margaret Theresa is wonderful with people who are dying . . . or think they're dying . . . (*gasps for breath, then blurts it out*) Dan and I . . . we sleep in the same bed. We're not like you and John.

ANN. Pardon?

BETSY. Don't you sleep in separate rooms?

ANN. Well, yes. Yes, most of the time now, yes. But that is mainly because John snores so loudly . . . it keeps me awake.

BETSY. I thought it was because of his drinking.

ANN. No. His snoring.

BETSY. Well, I want to still sleep with Dan in the same bed. *Still* . . . after thirteen years of marriage. I don't care if he snores . . . or breaks wind!

ANN. Betsy.

BETSY. I think he visits other women.

ANN. (*pause*) You're imagining things.

BETSY. Probably a buxom blonde with almond shaped eyes.

ANN. Nonsense.

BETSY. (*with sudden clarity*) I know he does. In my heart, I know it.

ANN. Don't be silly.

BETSY. I want him to love me.

ANN. He loves you. We know that. He's your husband.

BETSY. I mean in the dark. *In the dark!*

ANN. Shhhh.

BETSY. Is somebody listening? The children aren't here, they're at their grandmother's — Did John come in?

ANN. John will be late. They're having elections of new officers at the Knights of Columbus.

BETSY. Then why did you say "Shhhhhh"? Who's listening?

ANN. I am.

BETSY. Did I say something wrong? It's not wrong. I miss him touching . . . loving me . . . in the dark.

ANN. Betsy, you're thirty seven years old.

BETSY. I know my age. What has that to —

ANN. Dan's what . . . forty? Those romantic moments recede.

BETSY. Thirty seven isn't old.

ANN. *Now* you're a mother *first.*

BETSY. I'm what?

ANN. You're a mother first and a wife second and . . . (*at a loss for words*)

BETSY. And *myself third*?

ANN. (*shrugs*) That's the way it is. One has to accept that. (*BETSY begins to cry again.*)

CONNIE. (*entering*) I didn't ring the bell. I just walked . . . back in. Not backwards. (*illustrates*) But frontwards. (*Illustrates, but her kidding around doesn't pacify a distraught BETSY.*)

ANN. What did you forget?

CONNIE. (*to BETSY*) I had a feeling that you might

need a ride home after all.

BETSY. Oh, Connie, I am so unhappy.

ANN. I'll make you some hot tea. Some hot tea will do you good.

BETSY. I don't want any tea, thank you.

ANN. Betsy, some hot tea will do you the world of good, won't it, Connie?

BETSY. I don't want any—

CONNIE. It will do you good, Betsy.

BETSY. I'd like some ginger ale.

ANN. I think—

CONNIE. Ginger ale is almost as good as hot tea, Ann. (*ANN hesitates, then exits.*)

BETSY. Dan is . . . I think he visits other women.

CONNIE. (*pause*) Oh.

BETSY. He acts as if I'm not sleeping in the same bed with him anymore.

CONNIE. And how does he do that?

BETSY. What?

CONNIE. How does he make believe that you're not there?

BETSY. By lying still. By staying on his side of the bed, almost on the edge, sleeping on his side facing away from me. How would you feel if David did that to you?

CONNIE. He can't.

BETSY. He can't?

CONNIE. We have twin beds. (*pause*) Twin beds might be a solution

BETSY. What are you telling me?

CONNIE. You sleep better with twin beds. I do. David does.

BETSY. I love to snuggle up to Dan. Close. To his back.

CONNIE. Alice has twin beds, too.

BETSY. Keep them. Both of you. All of you. (*sudden revelation*) Did you get twin beds to punish your David? Because of his secretary? Dan said — (*shakes her head*) I don't want to punish Dan, I don't want to punish myself. (*pause*) I'm talking about *love*.

ANN. (*returning*) Here's your ginger ale.

BETSY. Thank you. (*pause*) I don't want twin beds.

CONNIE. Drink up.

ANN. I'm glad you're feeling better. It's good that Connie did come back. She can give you a ride home. Don't shake you head. You're in no mood to walk in the dark tonight. Freshen up now and powder your nose. (*gives her her purse, takes glass*)

BETSY. I look awful . . . because I was crying?

ANN. There's no need to have little Mary Lou broadcasting to the whole neighborhood that you've been upset.

BETSY. Mary Lou's stutter bothers her so that she barely talks. She's very sweet.

CONNIE. Go and freshen up, Betsy.

BETSY. (*suddenly sits in the nearest chair, grips the chair tightly, letting her purse fall*) I'm not going home tonight. I'm staying here.

ANN. You can't.

BETSY. I'll sleep in the den.

ANN. John sleeps in the den.

BETSY. Then I'll sit in this chair all night long.

ANN. People don't sit in chairs all night long.

CONNIE. Kathleen and Danny need you.

BETSY. Let Dan take care of them when he gets in at one or two or —

ANN. You *must* go home. You're responsible. Little Mary Lou can't —

BETSY. You're not my favorite sister anymore. (*rises*) Connie, I'll stay with you tonight.

CONNIE. You can't. The boys have a thousand friends staying for the weekend. I couldn't handle a thousand and one.

BETSY. Oh.

CONNIE. Come on, Betsy. I'll drive you home.

ANN. Put on your hat and powder your nose.

BETSY. Connie, I'll walk.

CONNIE. You silly goose . . . I'll give you a ride home.

ANN. Go on, Betsy.

BETSY. (*starts into the hall, hesitates*) When he comes home from work now he kisses me on the cheek. He seldom kisses me on the mouth anymore. I love his sweet mouth on mine. (*pause*) I'm sorry if I'm embarrassing you. Both of you. (*She exits into the hallway. CONNIE and ANN immediately move close together to confer, far from the hallway where BETSY is putting on her hat in front of the hallway mirror.*)

ANN. I'm so glad you came back. I had no idea what to say to her.

CONNIE. I suggested that she get twin beds.

ANN. (*getting more confidential*) I suggested that she talk with Sister Margaret Theresa.

CONNIE. Oh, boy. (*pause*) Sister Margaret Theresa would most likely tell her to take hot baths. Daily.

ANN. That's not funny.

CONNIE. It's not meant to be. I'm sure she would.

ANN. We can pray for her, Connie. We can both pray to St. Jude.

CONNIE. St. Jude. Martha's already bending his ear.

BETSY. (*returning*) Connie! Connie, who's *your* favorite sister?

ANN. Connie doesn't have a favorite sister either, do—

CONNIE. Yes, I do. I have one for every day of the week.

BETSY. What day am I?

CONNIE. You're Monday.

BETSY. Oh. *Blue* Monday . . .

ANN. (*picking up BETSY's coat*) Oh, Betsy, you don't get blue, oh, maybe a little pensive now and then, but—

CONNIE. None of us are perfect.

ANN. I am.

CONNIE. Except Ann.

ANN. Thank you.

CONNIE. Shall we— (*BETSY rushes off into the hall.*) What are you doing?

BETSY. (*from the hallway*) I just remembered.

ANN. (*almost to herself*) What now?

BETSY. (*returns with a blanket*) When you were hanging up my coat . . . I saw this on the shelf.

ANN. That's one of my best. I keep it in the front hall closet for—

CONNIE. What are you doing?

BETSY. I'm going to make a house. (*moves the four straight backed dining room chairs closer together*)

ANN. Betsy, it's a little late.

BETSY. It'll be fun!

CONNIE. It's late. Let's go home.

ANN. Betsy, really!

CONNIE. Come on, Betsy.

BETSY. (*to ANN*) Fix that end, Ann. (*growing more exuberant*) Just like you used to make them with me . . . when I was knee high to a grasshopper.

CONNIE. We're middle aged women now, you silly goose.

BETSY. Well, I'm not old. I'm lucky not to be as old as you two. (*gets down on the rug and moves into her tented house*) Oh, oh, it's wonderful! Please come under with me into my house. (*CONNIE and ANN stare helplessly at one another.*) If you don't I won't ride home with you, Connie . . . and if I walk in the dark, black night I might get raped.

ANN. Don't talk like that.

BETSY. Or get carried away by a white slaver.

CONNIE. Come out of there and I'll drive you home.

BETSY. If you both don't come under right now I'll have a nervous breakdown . . . or I'll cry and scream. Loud. The neighbors will hear, Ann.

ANN. I think Poppa should've spanked you more.

BETSY. Poppa and Mama never spanked me. Martha did it.

CONNIE. Come on out, you silly goose.

BETSY. (*pops her head out*) If I have a nervous breakdown there won't be any more Octette Bridge Club. (*She retreats. ANN and CONNIE exchange uneasy glances, then give up, get to giggling and join BETSY.*)

CONNIE. (*entering the blanket house*) We're as cuckoo as you are to do this.

BETSY. I'm not cuckoo. You said I wasn't. Isn't it cozy?

ANN. (*entering*) Ridiculous. (*and giggles*)

BETSY. (*overjoyed*) I love it! I love it better with you two beside me. (*CONNIE cackles.*) Now. We'll say a prayer, she said to pray to the Blessed Virgin Mary. She's partial to auburn haired women.

CONNIE. The Blessed Virgin Mary is partial to what?

BETSY. Auburn haired women. Like me.
CONNIE. Who said that? Nannette La Massney?
ANN. No. Madame Gambino.
CONNIE. (*pause*) Who?
ANN. Just pray . . . or we'll be here all night.
BETSY and CONNIE and ANN.
"Hail Mary, full of grace
The Lord is with thee
Blessed art thou amongst women
And blessed is the fruit of thy womb, Jesus . . ."

(*Lights fade to blackout*)

ACT TWO

Scene 1

TIME: *The night before Halloween, 1944. Ten years later.*

PLACE: *The same, ANN's living room. A few added pieces of furniture which makes the room a little more cluttered. There are new slipcovers, a new radio console, a piano bench has replaced the piano stool. And now on the wall is an 8x10 framed photograph of the Octette Bridge Club taken in 1934. The card tables are set up in different positions. At the upstage card table sitting clockwise: ANN, MARTHA, BETSY, LIL. At the downstage card table sitting clockwise: NORA, CONNIE, ALICE, MARY.*

In addition to Halloween decorations, they are all dressed at this time, in the Halloween tradition. They are costumed as follows:

ANN........................Queen of the Nile
MARTHA.......A Senorita (mantilla and shawl)
MARY........................Pilgrim Woman
NORA...............A Witch (with orange hat)
CONNIE.......................Another Witch
                    (with a black hat and fright wig)
ALICE.....................The Lone Ranger
LIL........................Red Riding Hood
BETSY .... Salome

With the exception of LIL, BETSY and ANN the costumes should be simple.

AS LIGHTS RISE: *We are in the midst of a hand. ANN is the dummy at her table and stands by her chair, watching . . . while CONNIE, the dummy at her table, is stretched out on the floor, her knees raised, her witch hat resting on her stomach. She has terrible back trouble, and when walking is forced to move about almost like a gorilla. Also, MARY is seated in a wheelchair, and her speech is slightly impaired due to a second stroke. MARTHA appears much older due to a recent operation. She limps, walks with a cane and now needs a hearing aid. LIL is larger and more jolly. BETSY is slimmer and more striking. The top of her costume is covered by a sweater. Silence.*

ALICE. Wasn't that terrible about Roland La Massney.

MARY. Terrible.

ANN. Oh, it was, God rest his soul.

ALICE. (*overlapping*) God rest his soul.

ANN. But it was Sister Margaret Theresa—God rest her soul, too—

ALICE. God rest her soul, too.

ANN. —that made me so sad.

MARTHA. What? Did they both pass away?

ALICE. (*louder*) You know, Martha. We told you.

MARTHA. What? What did you tell me that I don't know?

ALICE. Nannette La Massney stabbed her husband to death, and then she stabbed Sister Margaret Theresa to death.

MARTHA. God in Heaven!

LIL. Did you ever?!

MARY. True.

ALICE. Nannette claimed that they were having a clandestine relationship.

LIL. Who's Nannette La Massney?

ALICE. You remember Nannette La Massney. They owned La Massney's in Jericho, the stationery store. After Pearl Harbor, it become that USO canteen.

MARTHA. Both Roland La Massney and Sister Margaret Theresa?

ALICE. Both.

MARTHA. God rest their souls.

ALL. God rest their souls.

BETSY. It wasn't intentional. Nannette didn't do it intentionally.

MARTHA. How do you know?

BETSY. Because she told me.

MARTHA. She *told* you? Face to face?

BETSY. Yes. Twice a week I go back to Quidnekka Hall—

ANN. Betsy, that's in the past.

BETSY. Twice a week I go back to Quidnekka Hall to meet with Dr. Chisholm, and yesterday, after I visited my friend, Edith Leighton—She has visions—well, there was Nannette, already transferred to the first floor so she's making rapid progress. She asked for all of you. (*There is a slight uncomfortable mumbled response.*)

MARTHA. How could you even talk to her after she killed two people in cold blood?

BETSY. She's sorry. And she wasn't herself at the time. They call it a detoured focus or a diffusion of sanity.

ALICE. Roland La Massney always did have a cornucopia of lady friends . . . but this time, I believe, he was guiltless. He had just returned home from a gall bladder operation. Nannette, apparently, *had* been *herself* for years—

BETSY. Three years.

ALICE. —three years, until he came home from the hospital. But the minute Roland got home she was, apparently, *not* herself and began accusing him of philandering.

NORA. Philandering? After a gall bladder operation?

CONNIE. That doesn't make much sense, does it.

MARTHA. (*in reference to the game*) Play a card, Lil.

ALICE. So Roland called on that good old scout, Sister Margaret Theresa, who was always expert in affairs of the heart.

MARY. True.

BETSY. False. Sister Margaret Theresa never knew beans about sex.

ANN. Betsy.

BETSY. Ann suggested I go and see her—oh, years ago, ten years ago—when I suspected Dan of unfaithfulness and do you know what she told me to do?

CONNIE. Take hot baths. Daily.

BETSY. Exactly.

LIL. Did you ever. . .?!

BETSY. What I can't believe is how Nannette La Massney with her common sense could possibly think that her husband and Sister Margaret Theresa were having intercourse.

MARTHA and ANN. Betsy.

BETSY. That's what it's called, Martha. Dr. Chisholm said I should accept the word and use it in my vocabulary.

CONNIE. Sister Margaret Theresa always looked like a frog who wore glasses.

ANN. Connie, she's in her grave.

CONNIE. Well, she did.

MARTHA. God rest her soul.

OTHERS. God rest her soul.

ALICE. Let's remember that she was a bride of Christ.

CONNIE. Who else would marry her?

ANN. (*to CONNIE*) You are so bad.

MARTHA. What? What did she say?

CONNIE. Oh, Martha, turn up your hearing aid!

MARTHA. (*louder*) Don't shout! It's up, it's up! (*half to herself*) This little button sometimes sticks. What did she say?

CONNIE. I said, Happy Thirteenth Anniversary to us. Aren't we splendid!

MARTHA. You did not say that.

ALICE. (*overlapping*) Are you comfortable, Mary?

MARY. You worry about me too much, Alice.

ALICE. It's no bother to worry about you. (*to OTHERS*) The doctor says Mary's doing fine.

MARY. Isn't it nice to have Betsy back with us?

ALICE. Oh, yes, it is. (*They all add their approval.*)

MARY. So nice, Betsy. (*BETSY blows her a kiss.*) Betsy blew me a kiss. I caught it. Thank you, Betsy.

BETSY. You're welcome, Mary.

ANN. Connie, why don't you go into my bedroom and stretch out for a bit?

CONNIE. No, this is fine. It got so bad last night I slept on the floor.

ANN. I thought you put a board under your mattress?

CONNIE. I did. But the floor is so much better. David came down and slept beside me.

MARTHA. On the floor?

CONNIE. Yes!

NORA. Wasn't that nice of him.

CONNIE. And he held my hand . . . like we were young . . . through the night.

ANN. Can I get you a pillow?

CONNIE. Stop fretting. I want to stay here where I won't miss anything. Besides, I have to advise my partner.

MARY. Partner. You're a lot of help down there, lazybones.

CONNIE. Isn't she getting saucy in her Pilgrim outfit? I think she's been off in the woods with John Alden.

MARY. You'd be surprised.

LIL. Oh, sugar.

ANN. Oh, my goodness, Betsy. You've become a whirlwind.

BETSY. I played a lot at Quidnekka Hall.

ANN. You're here now.

LIL. Ann, what is the prize for the best costume?

ANN. When the winner wins, you'll see the prize. Later.

LIL. Nora, you and Connie will be knocked out of the competition because you both came dressed the same.

CONNIE. You be careful, Lil, or we'll put a curse on you.

ALICE. Which one of you is the *bad* witch?

NORA. We're not telling.

MARTHA. Let Connie be the bad witch. It suits her better. (*laughter*)

ALICE. Is that so! Well, what about Nora and the cemetery, All Saints Day, back when in 1934?

MARTHA. Oh! Oh, yes!

MARY. Oh, dear.	LIL. Ohhhhh.	ANN. Let's drop the subject.

MARTHA. Oh, yes! — Up at the crack of dawn, so you and your boys could have your outing, oh, yes!

NORA. To tell you the truth, Martha, that morning delighted me because for once you couldn't run the show your way.

MARTHA. Well. . . !	LIL. Did you ever. . . ?	ANN. Let's drop the subject.

BETSY. (*unintentionally*) Oh, shit. (*sudden silence*) Oops.

MARTHA. Did you swear? (*pause*) Did she swear? (*ALICE and LIL nod.*)

CONNIE. Sounded to me like Betsy had a slight, a *very* slight diffusion of sanity . . . or a detoured focus, right, Betsy?

BETSY. Right, Connie.

CONNIE. (*cackles*) I like that. Detoured focus. I wonder if I'll ever have one of those. What do you think, Betsy?

ANN. (*quickly*) Are you sure you don't want a pillow?

CONNIE. Nooo! Stop. This is the way it's supposed to be. Head flat on the floor. It helps.

ANN. Did you see that other specialist?

CONNIE. Dr. Horowitz . . . same as the rest. A slipped disc eccentricity that will remain with me for the rest of my life . . . go away of its own accord . . . or kill me.

ANN. It will go away. I pray for you, you know that.

MARTHA. We all do.

BETSY. Everybody prays for me, too, Connie.

ANN. Of course.

CONNIE. Aren't we lucky?

BETSY. Hooray!

ANN. Did we win that hand?

BETSY. Yes, we did. Whoopee!

ANN. Oh, good.

MARY. We did, too, Connie.

CONNIE. Hubba! Hubba!

MARY. We gave Nora and Alice such a skunking, Connie.

ALICE. You did not.

LIL. Time to change tables.

CONNIE. Which means it is time for my resurrection.

NORA. Looks that way.

CONNIE. Oh, well. Up and at'em.

LIL. (*moving quickly, checking MARY's score*) High's here . . . low's there. Then we'll draw for new partners.

BETSY. I'm over there. You, too, Ann.

NORA. You're at the other table, Alice.

LIL. Connie . . . Connie, you're with us over here. (*BETSY has moved to the picture of the "Octette" on the wall. ANN has moved to the "high" table.*)

ANN. Easy, Connie.

(*And through the following CONNIE continues her ritual, a slow painful process of rising into an apelike position, finally moving to her chair, leaning on it for support, and eventually sitting.*)

CONNIE. The other day I was out in the backyard hanging my corset out on the line to air out . . . and the little boy, Wayne, from next door came over. He asked me why I walked like a gorilla. I told him I had back trouble. He said his grandmother had back trouble but she didn't walk like a gorilla. I told him his grandmother walked like a penguin. He said he thought so, too . . . and did we laugh! . . . and off he went. About an hour later, I went out back to get my corset *off* the line, reached up, lost my balance and flopped back on my behind. I sat there, I couldn't get up, don't ask me why . . . like being paralyzed, I just couldn't get up for the life of me. It started to drizzle. I had the corset in my hand so I put it over my head for protection and I shouted: "Help! Help!" . . . waited . . . hummed songs . . . prayed for my boys. Next thing you know the corset's being lifted by Wayne's mother. "Mrs. Emerson, did you tell Wayne that his grandmother walks like a penguin?" I said: "Yes, I did." She said she thought it was a terrible thing to say to a boy his age, and I said he said I walked like a gorilla and she said: "You do!" . . . honest. And I said: "I walk like a gorilla because it pains me to waddle like a penguin. Now would you please help me to my feet and give me back my gosh darn corset!"

LIL. Did you ever?!

ALICE. I don't believe that story.

CONNIE. Do I lie?

BETSY. What happened? What did she do?

CONNIE. She helped me to my feet, handed me my corset, and told me that she forbade Wayne to come into my yard again.

MARTHA. Why did you say such an awful thing about his grandmother?

CONNIE. Because he made me mad.

MARTHA. A child?

CONNIE. Yes, a child.

MARTHA. You could exercise a little self control.

BETSY. Self control can eat you alive.

CONNIE. Hear that, Martha?

MARTHA. Am I to surmise that you have become an expert on self control?

BETSY. You may surmise that, if you like.

NORA. Draw, Mary.

ANN. At least she gave you your corset back. Betsy.

CONNIE. I wanted to hit her with it.

LIL. Draw, Martha.

BETSY. Why didn't you?

CONNIE. I'm a lady.

NORA. Come draw, Betsy.

MARTHA. Betsy, go and draw.

BETSY. (*a slight flare*) I'm going, Martha.

MARTHA. (*pause*) I have told you, forever and a day, that I don't like that look. (*BETSY hesitates, the OTHERS turn to her, but she doesn't respond to MARTHA, moves to the table and draws.*)

NORA. Oh, we're partners, Betsy. Good. (*They now have new partners and move to new positions at each table. At table right will soon be: CONNIE, MARTHA, LIL, ALICE . . . at table left: NORA, ANN, BETSY, MARY.*)

LIL. It's you and me, Connie. Oh! Do you know what we could do before we start the next rubber? We could get down on our knees and say a prayer together for all our boys overseas! . . . in Europe, in the Far East, wherever . . . and especially our own kind.

ANN. I think that is a wonderful idea.

LIL. Isn't it?   MARY. Yes.   ALICE. It is.

NORA. (*overlapping*)   MARTHA. (*overlapping*)
That's wonderful.   Oh, yes. Yes.

LIL. Connie, you don't have to get down on your knees . . . or you, Martha.

MARTHA. Of course I will.

CONNIE. I certainly will. I may wind up on all fours . . . but God will know what I'm intending. Right, God? Right. (*All begin to kneel.*)

LIL. We'll pray that our own will come home safe and sound, and with all their faculties — No offense, Betsy —

CONNIE. Start, Lil, before I fall over.

LIL. (*finally kneeling*) We offer this prayer, O Lord, particularly for our own kind . . . Connie's four sons . . .

CONNIE. David, Philip, William, and Kevin.

LIL. . . . Nora's two sons . . .

NORA. Lawrence and Thomas, watch over them.

ANN. My boy Teddy.

BETSY. My son Danny. May he come back from the

Navy with all his . . . safe and sound . . . and not be ashamed of his mother because she was away at Quidnekka Hall. God bless him and God bless me.

MARTHA. Betsy, Betsy, Betsy . . . we're not praying for ourselves, we are—

BETSY. If I want to pray for "ourselves" along with my own son and all my nephews, I *will.* I don't think any one in this room should object to the way I pray. Least of all you. You have four daughters and none of them are in the Army, Navy or the Marines so you pray *your* way and I'll pray mine.

MARTHA. (*pause*) I'm beginning to find conversation with you a bit trying.

CONNIE. Lil, if you don't start this darn prayer I am going to wring your neck!

ANN. Lil, maybe it would be better if each of us offered up a minute of silent prayer like we—

LIL. Yes, silent.

CONNIE. Honestly.

LIL. Starting now. Go! (*And she makes the sign of the cross, OTHERS do the same. Silence. They all close their eyes and pray. Some are mouthing words of prayers. MARTHA opens her eyes and steals a glance at BETSY, glaring at her with disapproval. BETSY, conscious of being stared at, opens her eyes and turns to MARTHA who immediately turns away, again closing her eyes and continuing her fervent prayer. Finishing with another sign of the cross:*) There!

ALICE. That wasn't a minute.

CONNIE. It was close enough.

NORA. What a good idea that was, Lil. (*There are a few moans and groans as they slowly get to their feet.*)

BETSY. I wonder if the Octette Bridge Club will outlast the war.

MARTHA. You're full of pleasant thoughts.

(*LIL, on her feet, in a sudden outburst, begins singing a patriotic song. OTHERS, joining her in the song, are returning to their seats. LIL gets herself into a real marching spirit, including a salute or two. LIL finishes the song. There is a little applause. CONNIE is dealing, NORA is dealing.*)

CONNIE. Quick! Back to the game . . . or Lil will lead us into a chorus of The Battle Hymn of the Re—

MARTHA. Isn't she sassy.

LIL. (*sings*) *"Mine eyes have seen the glory of the coming of the Lord . . ."* (*They all howl with laughter. It's like old times. In a higher range, still singing:*) Play cards! Play cards!

ALICE. Then sit down.

ANN. All right, everyone concentrate. Back to important business.

NORA. Back to important business.

CONNIE. Here! Here! (*They quiet down.*)

LIL. *God Bless America* should be our National Anthem.

BETSY. Isn't it?

LIL. No, Betsy, it isn't. You know it isn't. Don't you? Doesn't she?

ALICE. Of course she knows it isn't. *The Star Spangled Banner* is.

LIL. *The Star Spangled Banner* is very hard to sing.

ALICE. Isn't it.

NORA. I pass.

LIL. (*overlapping*) It really is. (*sings*) *"Oh, say, can you—"*

CONNIE. Don't you dare! One club. (*LIL giggles.*)

ANN. One diamond.

MARTHA. Pass.

BETSY. I thought they changed it to *God Bless America* because of the war. One spade.

ALICE. No, Betsy, they didn't. You know they didn't. Don't you? Doesn't she?

LIL. They should change it. Pass.

MARTHA. No, they shouldn't.

MARY. Two diamonds.

MARTHA. Let it remain as it is.

ALICE. One No Trump.

MARTHA. Keep things as they are.

NORA. Two hearts.

ANN. Three diamonds.

CONNIE. Two clubs.

MARTHA. Pass. We need roots.

LIL. Pass.

MARTHA. People need roots.

ALICE. Two no Trump.

MARTHA. Traditions.

BETSY. Three hearts.

MARTHA. Security

CONNIE. Pass.

MARTHA. Honor.

MARY. Pass.

CONNIE. Are you planning to run for governor, Martha?

MARTHA. *Pass.*

NORA. Three spades.

LIL. Pass.

ALICE. Two No Trump it is!

ANN. Pass.

MARTHA. All I'm saying is that there is enough turmoil now with the war without changing other things . . . especially the National Anthem.

LIL. You're the dummy, Martha.

MARTHA. I know.

ALICE. Two No Trump it is!

MARTHA. I heard you.

BETSY. I'm just sorry that I wasn't home to cook my boy's breakfast the morning he left for the Navy.

ANN. You don't have to feel guilty about that. Bid, Betsy.

BETSY. I don't feel guilty. I feel sorry. Danny loves blueberry pancakes. I would've made them for him.

ANN. Betsy, bid.

BETSY. Four spades.

MARY. Pass.

NORA. Pass.   ANN. Pass.

BETSY. It's ours, Nora.

ALICE. Are you comfortable, Mary?

MARY. Fine, Alice, fine, dear.

(*MARTHA, using her cane, has risen and moves about during the following, halfheartedly checking the hands of the various players, now a rather restrained overseer.*)

CONNIE. Do you know what else I was thinking when I was sitting out there in the rain with the corset over my head? I was thinking: You hardly ever read anything anymore about the Dionne Quintuplets.

BETSY. That's because they're midgets.

LIL. Are you crazy? Oh, I'm sorry. I'm sorry, Betsy.

MARTHA. Isn't this pretty? Michael gave me this shawl

when we were first married. I never wore it. Too frivo-
lous. Now I wear it.

ALICE. (*loudly*) It looks lovely.

MARTHA. Stop shouting at me, Alice.

ALICE. I didn't shout, dear. I just raised my voice.

MARTHA. I'm not deaf.

ALICE. (*softly to Connie*) Did I shout?

ANN. (*overlapping*) Remember now, in addition to
the costume, each of us has to do a little show for the
prize. Same rules as last year.

LIL. (*singing*) "*I'm the Halloween girl, I'm the Halloween pearl . . .*"

MARTHA. (*overlapping; near NORA's chair*) Has
Larry got used to his hearing aid?

NORA. No. He hates to wear it . . . but he says it helps.

MARTHA. I hate it, too. But I agree with him . . . it
helps. You're the dummy, too. Come and talk with me.

NORA. He says it makes him realize that he's not
twenty anymore.

MARY. You and Larry always act like you're twenty.

NORA. We do not. We're very dignified.

MARY. You're still love birds.

LIL. Tweet, tweet, tweet! (*giggly responses*)

MARTHA. (*as she sits*) You do still love him.

NORA. Of course I do. I loved him the first time he
kissed me. (*She joins MARTHA, sits. She gets some
"ooooos" and "ahhhhhs."*)

MARTHA. On the front porch, I remember. I was
behind the screen door. I reported to Mama, Mama
reported to Poppa.

NORA. After, you scolded me . . . told me I shouldn't
let any young man kiss me. So bossy.

MARTHA. I was the oldest. I was trained to be bossy.
There was a houseful of babies.

LIL. Like me.   ALICE. Like me.

MARY. Like you, Betsy.

MARTHA. (*overlapping*) That evening after I scolded you you said you wanted him to kiss you for the rest of your life.

NORA. Uh huh. And he did. He still does.

MARTHA. Sweet.

MARY. Love birds!

LIL. Tweet, tweet, tweet!   OTHERS. (*more emphatic*) "Ooooooos" and "Ahhhhhhhs"

NORA. (*lightly*) Oh, stop it, all of you. (*rising*) Can I get you something, Martha? Some ginger ale?

MARTHA. No. Sit, Nora.

ANN. I have your favorite, dear. Canada Dry.

MARTHA. A few years ago I was shopping in Jericho, Christmastime. I saw a man and a woman ahead of me in the street. They were holding hands. I remember thinking: Look at them, at their age, holding hands, behaving like children. And then the couple stopped, and turned to look in a store window. You were the couple, Nora, you and Larry. I didn't approach you, turned and hurried back to my car . . . got in behind the wheel . . . didn't move, couldn't, couldn't start the motor, just sat and began to shake, angry with Michael for dying and leaving me a widow with four daughters to raise. I'd leaned on the horn. Somebody knocked on the window. I rolled it down. A man with a handlebar moustache like Michael's, asked me if anything was wrong. I said, "Yes" and he asked, "What?" I told him none of his business and I spit right in his face. (*pause*) I was so ashamed. I'd never done anything so terrible in my life. (*By now she has everyone's attention.*)

NORA. What did he do?

MARTHA. He spit right back.

CONNIE. (*cackles*) Good for him.

MARTHA. Did I sound self pitying? I didn't, did I? I didn't.

BETSY. Laugh and the world laughs with you, cry and you cry alone.

ALICE and MARY. (*overlapping*) —cry and you cry alone.

MARTHA. (*quickly overcoming her embarrassment; slightly defensive*) What I meant to say, before I got sidetracked, was that Nora did the best of us in the husband department.

NORA. Thank you. I think so, too.

LIL. You did not. I did.

CONNIE. You did not. Peter's so short.

LIL. I'll bop you one.

BETSY. I think Dan is the best husband right now. He's been so kind.

ALICE. Oh, yes, yes, he has.　　MARY. True.

BETSY. Very considerate.

ANN. Oh, yes, he is.

BETSY. (*impulsively rises*) At Quidnekka Hall he came to visit me every day. Oh, not that first month . . . but the following four months.

NORA. And it's such a long drive, back and forth.

ALICE and MARY. True.　　LIL. It is.

BETSY. I appreciated his coming every day.

ANN. Shall we finish this hand?

BETSY. And since I've come back from there, and with the continuing help of Dr. Chisholm, I'm beginning to learn courage. I didn't know I had any. But I do.

ANN. Shall we?

BETSY. (*Her speech is more hurried.*) Since I've come home, I've tried to take some small steps . . . have the courage to say what I think . . . make changes. I told Dan that I would no longer iron his shirts. They would have to go to the laundry, and he would have to take them there himself. (*They are stunned.*)

NORA. What did he say to that?

BETSY. He said: "All right."

LIL. He did?

BETSY. He did! But he asked why. I said because I want some time to think about doing some reading, or maybe going to college . . .

ANN. College? At your age?

CONNIE. Shhhhhh.

BETSY. And I told Dan how I wanted to sleep in the same bed with him again, and we did. And we were intimate and it was . . . it was . . . heavenly.

MARY. Heavenly is nice, Betsy.

BETSY. Yes, Mary, it is.

MARTHA. That is enough of that.

BETSY. Let me finish, Martha, please. It isn't easy but I need to say it out loud, I need to let you all know that I want to change, I want to be healthy.

MARTHA. Go on! Go on, go on, go on, go on! Don't let me stop you. Go on, go on.

BETSY. (*pause*) But sharing the same bed again doesn't remove the long time problem. I told Dan that I would no longer put up with his shenanigans with other women and if he couldn't halt his shenanigans then I wanted a separation, I wanted him to live elsewhere. (*They are more stunned.*)

CONNIE. What did he say to that?

BETSY. He looked at me as if he'd been shot . . . which, through the years, I thought a lot about doing . . . but I never had a gun.

LIL. But what did he say?

BETSY. He said: "Is there any more pie?" And I said: "Help yourself."

ALICE. You didn't.

BETSY. I did. (*breathless*) I have more to say, but I can't right now. I'll try later. (*sits; silence*)

LIL. What kind of pie?

Blackout

SCENE 2

TIME: *About an hour later.*

BEFORE LIGHTS RISE: *We hear, on the piano, "The Lone Ranger" theme music (The* William Tell Overture*). Some are humming along with the piano music.*

AS LIGHTS RISE: *ALICE, wearing the mask now, is center, galloping about on an invisible horse. LIL, through the following mini-shows, is compelled to give everybody accompaniment, vocally or at the piano, sometimes a bit of both. She gets good vocal assistance and sound effects from CONNIE. Remains of refreshments are about.*

ALICE. I am the Lone Ranger, as you can see. (*She shoots LIL at the piano. LIL, shot, collapses on the piano keys. Applause.*) And I see before me seven damsels in distress.

LIL. We've lost our father, Lone Ranger.

CONNIE. And our mother, Lone Ranger.

ALICE. I'll find them for you.

ANN. You'll only find them if you have the key to Heaven.

ALICE. Oh, I can find that all right . . . and when I do, I will go into Heaven and tell your father and mother that you love them and miss them . . . but are *not* too anxious to join them. Hi yo, Silver! Awayyyyyyyyyy!

(*She slaps her thigh, gallops about the room to much hoopla and exits. They laugh and applaud wildly. Through the following we must clearly see that they permit one another to make fools of themselves. There is a freedom, then, in this kind of hi-jinks for them.*)

ALICE. (*returns, moving her mask above her forehead*) You're next, Mary.

MARTHA. No, I'll be next. I want to get it over with . . . (*hobbles forward*) . . . before we get the more sophisticated strutters.

LIL. Like who?

MARTHA. Like you. I'd better win best prize. I might not see another Halloween . . . or Thanksgiving. (*hands out her cane, BETSY takes it*)

ANN. (*folding a card table to make more room for the "performers"*) Oh, Martha, you'll outlive us all.

MARTHA. (*clears her throat; with an accent*) I'm Senorita Rodriquez. (*Sashays with a hip, but it hurts.*) I come from south of the border. (*Group laughs.*) And I will play for you my castanets. (*steadies her stance, moves her hands and plays, with verbal clacking sounds, her castanets*) Ole! (*Wild applause follows and MARTHA reaches for her cane as BETSY quickly hands it to her.*)

ANN. Oh, you're all so much better than I was. Can I

do my Queen of the Nile again? (*She gets responses of "No" and hisses. ANN laughs and clangs two potlids together, then sets the potlids down. ALICE starts wheeling MARY forward.*) Oh, Mary, you don't have—

ALICE. She wants to.

MARY. I have to try and win.

NORA. Of course, you do. (*ALICE hushes them.*)

MARY. I am . . . Pilgrim Woman. I live in a nice log cabin with my nice husband, Pilgrim Man . . . who is a hunter . . . and my nice dog, Spot . . . who is a dog. *And* my nice turkeys.

ALICE. Do you have names for your turkeys, Pilgrim Woman?

MARY. Oh, yes. Turkey One, Turkey Two, Turkey Three—

CONNIE. (*falsetto*) Turkey Four . . .

ALICE. And what did you do this morning, Pilgrim Woman?

MARY. This morning I went out to feed the turkeys. Turkey Two came over and pecked at my skirt.

ALICE. What did he say?

CONNIE. Gobble! Gobble!

MARY. No. No. He said not to kill him next month for Thanksgiving because he was . . . dreaming of a white Christmas. (*They all sigh, appreciative.*) The end. (*applause*) Wasn't I good? With all my trouble talking, too . . . wasn't I good, Alice?

ALICE. You were wonderful.

MARY. I remembered everything.

NORA. You were wonderful, Mary.

MARTHA. Where's my ginger ale?

ANN. What about you, Betsy? (*And through the following ANN begins to distribute pencil and paper to each of them.*)

BETSY. No, no, I want to be last.

LIL. *I* want to be last. (*ALICE wheels MARY out of the way.*)

MARTHA. Has anyone seen my ginger ale?

CONNIE. (*overlapping*) Nora and I will go.

NORA. Our turn.

ANN. It's right there where you left it, Martha, right in front of you, dear.

CONNIE. (*overlapping*) Shhh.

MARTHA. Oh, I'm going blind, too. Deaf, dumb and blind.

CONNIE. Quiet, please.

MARTHA. Well, at least, I'm not dumb. Not quite yet.

CONNIE. Martha, will you zip your lip.

NORA. (*joining CONNIE*) Shhhh. A Poem!

NORA and CONNIE. By us!

CONNIE. There once were two witches named—

NORA. Nora.

CONNIE. —and Connie.

NORA. I was very, very bad . . .

CONNIE. And I had lots of money.

NORA and CONNIE.

And off to Germany we did fly

Over Hitler's marble swastikas, it's no lie

And with our magic broomsticks there we stood

And whacked that Hitler man good

And, oh, how we glowed

For we turned him into a toad

And they all ran away down the road

For who in the heck would say: "Heil, Toad!"

(*much response*)

So right away the war ended.

And all our boys came home mended.

(*More applause, laughter. CONNIE and NORA are bowing to one another.*)

ALICE. You're both good witches. You ended the war!

MARTHA. Weren't they cute.

ANN. (*continuing to pass out papers and pencils*) Who's next? Betsy.

BETSY. No, Ann. I want to be last. I said so.

LIL. I'd like to go last, Betsy.

BETSY. No, Lil.

ANN. Lil.

MARTHA. Being the youngest doesn't always entitle you to special privileges.

CONNIE. Martha, finish your ginger ale . . . dear.

NORA. Come on, Lil. (*goes to the piano to accompany LIL*)

LIL. Oh, all right, I'll go. I'm easy to get along with. (*pops up and poses*) Well, you all know who I am.

CONNIE. Betty Grable.

LIL. No. You know I'm not her. I am the one and only Little Red Riding Hood.

NORA. Ready, Lil?

LIL. Ready. (*She sings a song about Red Riding Hood. Much applause; LIL is full of bows.*)

NORA. You should've gone on the stage.

LIL. That's true.

ALICE. Lil, you are so inventive.

LIL. That's true, too.

ANN. Now, Betsy. Last, but not least.

BETSY. Last but not least. Lil, will you play for me? *Sheik of Araby* or music like that . . . with a vamp.

LIL. Are you going to sing or what?

BETSY. No, dance. Wait. I have to get my things. Just a minute. (*rushes off*)

NORA. Where's she going?

ANN. (*shrugging*) She came early. She brought two boxes with her and put them in the den. One was a hat box.

MARY. Who is she?

ALICE. Salome. That's what she said.

CONNIE. A hat box?

ANN. Yes.

CONNIE. She's got John the Baptist in there.

MARTHA. Oh, my Lord!

ANN. (*lowering her voice*) What should we do? Do you think we should let her win the costume prize?

(*And through the following they all begin to whisper:*)

LIL. *No.* We do it the way we've always done it. She says she wants to be healthy.

MARTHA. She's not herself.

NORA. She's only been home three weeks. Look what she's accomplished.

MARTHA. What?

NORA. She's doing fine.

ANN. Should we?

LIL. No.

ALICE. We should treat her the way we've always treated her.

CONNIE. Like the baby?

MARTHA. She's not herself.

NORA. She's doing fine.

ANN. (*even softer voiced*) We should let her win the prize.

ALICE. That would be hypocritical.

LIL. I agree.

MARY. She looks so pretty.

MARTHA. She's not herself.

NORA. She's doing fine.

BETSY. (*offstage*) All right, Lil! Start playing!

(*LIL begins to play, vamping. BETSY enters, barefooted. She has removed her sweater, now wearing seven colorful veils over her colorful skirt. Balancing John the Baptist on a tray on her head she slowly dances forward.*)

MARTHA. It is the head of John the Baptist.

CONNIE. He looks so tired. (*BETSY sets the tray down on the floor, and then her dancing becomes more exotic as LIL begins to play the chorus.*) Give the lady room! (*Pause. BETSY tosses a veil aside.*) Oh.

MARTHA. Oh.

CONNIE. Two!

ALICE. Oh, Betsy.

CONNIE. (*laughs a little now*) Three! You wild thing! (*And BETSY dances with more abandon.*) Four! (*Silence. BETSY's gyrations hold their attention.*) Five! Keep that tempo, Lil. She's inspired. Six! One to go!

ANN. Careful.

CONNIE. Seven! (*And the seventh veil has gone flying. BETSY is wearing a flimsy bra with two fringed tassels covering her breasts which she shakes vigorously and ends her dance with a slow slide to the floor. LIL coordinates on the piano with much flourish, and then gets up quickly to get a better view of BETSY. Silence. The unexpected. They are all speechless.*) Where did you get those tassels?

BETSY. From an old lampshade down cellar.

MARTHA. Cover yourself.

BETSY. What?

MARTHA. Gather your veils—Pick up your veils or whatever they are and cover yourself. (*BETSY remains still. ALICE and ANN begin to collect the veils.*)

MARY. (*amazed*) Did you learn that at Quidnekka Hall?

BETSY. Yes. A belly dancer, a Greek girl. I taught her how to play bridge. She taught me how to—

LIL. Shimmy and shake.

MARTHA. Cover yourself.

ALICE. Here, Betsy. (*gives veils to BETSY*)

CONNIE. I didn't know you had it in you.

MARTHA. That's not funny.

ANN. No, it isn't.

MARTHA. I said cover yourself.

ANN. (*handing her veils*) Here.

MARTHA. I've never seen such an exhibition . . . from any of us.

NORA. It's a costume.

ANN. Cover yourself. Put them on.

MARTHA. What kind of a place is that Quidnekka Hall? Belly dancing. Greeks.

BETSY. Jews, too.

ANN. Put them all on.

BETSY. I will.

MARTHA. Betsy-Betsy-Betsy.

BETSY. Oh, don't be such a crab apple, Martha. Oh, I know you're in pain but so is Mary and so is Connie and they're not crabby about it all the time.

MARTHA. Don't you dare talk to me in that tone of voice.

ALICE. It's time to vote for the best costume, isn't it, Ann?

ANN. Yes, you're right. You've all got pencil and paper. Just write your winner and we'll shake them up—

CONNIE. More shaking?

ANN. — Shake them up in Alice's hat — Use the other veils, too, Betsy — And remember, there's a prize.

CONNIE. What is it? The head of John the Baptist?

ANN. Fold them . . . just toss them into the Lone Ranger's hat. Thanks for the use of your hat.

ALICE. You're welcome. It's a worthy cause.

ANN. All right! All right! There! Oh, Betsy . . . (*moves to Betsy to collect her vote*) Thank you. There. Nora, would you do the honors, please? (*LIL makes an heraldic trumpeting sound.*)

NORA. (*drawing from the hat that ANN holds*) The Lone Ranger. (*cheers and applause*) Queen of the Nile. (*cheers and applause*) Red Riding Hood. (*cheers and applause*) Pilgrim Woman. (*cheers and applause*) Senorita from Mexico. (*cheers and applause*) Red Riding Hood. (*cheers and applause*) Pilgrim Woman. (*cheers and applause*) So far there is a tie.

ANN. Red Riding Hood . . . and Pilgrim Woman.

CONNIE. Go on. (*cheers and applause*)

NORA. And here's the last. Red Riding—

LIL. (*overlapping*) Oh, I won! I won!! (*jumps with joy*) Where's my prize?

ANN. (*laughing*) I'll get it. (*Exits. LIL sings a line or two of her song again.*)

CONNIE. You see, Nora? I told you. Nobody voted for us.

NORA. You could have voted for yourself.

BETSY. No one voted for me either.

CONNIE. Not one vote for Salome and the two witches. Wouldn't that make a nice children's story?

ANN. (*returning*) Here we are, Lil.

ALICE. Open it.

LIL. Of course I'll open it. If I didn't you'd all kill me.

Oh, what pretty wrapping, Ann.

MARY. Isn't it?

CONNIE. Let's hear it for the pretty wrapping!

ALL. Rah! Rah! Rah!

MARTHA. I wonder what it is.

LIL. (*getting it open*) Oh. It's . . . it's . . . what is it, Ann? Oh, it's. . . ?

ANN. Bubble bath. Evergreen. Little evergreen bubble bath balls.

CONNIE. (*pause*) Little evergreen bubble bath balls. Just what you needed, Lil.

LIL. Oh. I see.

CONNIE. Certainly Little Red Riding Hood needs a good evergreen bubble bath.

ANN. It's supposed to be very soothing. Evergreen.

BETSY. It is. They have wonderful evergreens at Quidnekka Hall. I took long walks most—

ANN. That time is over with! Stop bringing it up . . . it's unpleasant and it's over. Don't dwell on it.

BETSY. You're beginning to sound like Martha.

ANN. (*warmer*) It's in the past. You're well now. You're recovered. You're back with us . . . and that makes all of us happy. For five months there was no Octette Bridge Club.

LIL. If you keep talking about it again and again you have no choice but to remember sad things because it was a sad time for you. So let's be happy.

MARY. Yes.   ALICE. Please.

BETSY. But I want to be aware of what I went through. It was painful, but it was good. Quidnekka Hall helped me. Dr. Chisholm—

ANN. Betsy, you must remember . . . like I do . . . that it does no good to think about oneself too much. The best thing to do is—

BETSY. There's nothing wrong with thinking about yourself.

ANN. There are better things to do . . . such as utilizing that spare time, filling up that time with prayers for Danny off fighting for his country. I know that helps me.

BETSY. And do you fill up that spare time praying for your husband? Do you pray that he'll stop drinking?

ANN. (*taken aback*) Yes, I pray that his drinking will . . . lessen. Would anyone like any more tea or coffee or ginger ale? Cookies?

BETSY. I'm not even sure if I believe in God anymore.

ALICE. Of course you believe in God. We all do.

BETSY. In Quidnekka Hall—

MARTHA. That is enough. Stop talking about—

BETSY. (*determined*) In Quidnekka Hall, *in that hospital*, I thought a lot about us. And when things were dark and bad, I'd be glad that the Octette Bridge Club would go on and on . . . come rain or come shine . . .

LIL. Sleet or snow!

ALICE. War or peace!

BETSY. But us . . . we eight sisters . . . (*rising*) . . . I realized that we never talk to one another about anything serious.

LIL. We all talk too much . . . if you ask me.

BETSY. Sisters . . . but not close.

LIL. Let's have some songs.

ALICE. Oh, yes.

LIL. How about *Shine On Harvest Moon*? (*begins to play*)

BETSY. Can't I finish talking?

LIL. I'm trying to cheer you up.

BETSY. (*crossing to LIL*) You're trying to shut me up. (*LIL stops playing.*) I was so depressed . . . so unhappy . . . and I tried to —

ALICE. Betsy, don't.   MARTHA. *No.*

BETSY. I tried to commit suicide.

ALICE. This is our Thirteenth Anniversary. Don't spoil it.

BETSY. (*her courage growing*) I remember our third anniversary . . . ten years ago . . . here. That was the night the trouble started for me. Connie gave me a ride home, and I went inside, paid Mary Lou for babysitting, got my scissors from my sewing basket and I cut up the kitchen curtains I'd just made. And for . . . well, the next ten years . . . Doctor Carroll would call my . . . misbehaviors the flu . . . or nerves . . . and I'd be in bed for a week or two. Once I remember smashing all my Norataki China . . . Ann came over and helped me clean it up, and the next day I went to that psychiatrist who had such bad teeth and he gave me those pills that made me so groggy all the time. But every other Friday . . . the Octette Bridge Club was always something I looked forward to . . . safe. Oh, all of you seemed to think I was stupid, but —

NORA. No.

BETSY. I had the chance here to prove that I wasn't! I could win! I became something, a good bridge player . . . my claim to fame and fortune. (*pause*) I don't know why I did what I did. (*pause*) It was a beautiful day; and I was cleaning our room. When I finished I took Dan's pants and jackets and went out in the backyard and had a bonfire, and when everything was burned I went back inside and went into the bathroom and slashed my wrists.

ANN. Don't

MARTHA. You weren't yourself.

BETSY. Dan had to commit me . . . he didn't have much choice. But I wanted to go, I think I wanted to go years before. I needed help. (*pause; attempting to override her tears*) Why didn't you come to see me? Oh, you sent gifts and cards and flowers . . . but not one of you came to see me. My sisters. (*pause*) That hurt so much.

NORA. (*long pause*) The doctor said . . . Dan said . . . it was best that we didn't visit.

BETSY. That was only in the beginning, Nora, for the first month.

LIL. We didn't know what to do.

ALICE. We wanted to visit.

ANN. We thought it was best. All of us agreed, it was a mutual agreement. We went to mass together for you, we prayed for your quick recovery. Our prayers were answered.

CONNIE. Baloney! We didn't want anybody gossiping about the wonderful saintly Donavan girls . . . the scandal! . . . or anybody seeing us going in and out of Quidnekka Hall as if anybody would in Woonsocket. But when Martha had her operation we were there in full force. And when Mary had her stroke . . . we were there. But going inside *that* place? Quidnekka Hall? (*pause*) I guess we were all frightened. More baloney! No excuses . . . Pretty disgraceful conduct . . . all of us.

ANN. We agreed—

CONNIE. I know we agreed.

MARTHA. (*restrained*) It was majority rule.

CONNIE. And it was wrong. (*to BETSY*) I should've gone to visit you. We all should've. I'm ashamed.

NORA. So am I.

MARY. So am I.

LIL. Me, too. (*ANN, ALICE, and MARTHA nod reluctantly.*)

CONNIE. Can you forgive us?

BETSY. (*pause*) In time.

CONNIE. Alice has a new Bulova. Give her thirty seconds, Alice.

BETSY. More time than that.

CONNIE. Okay. We're patient.

BETSY. What I wanted to say earlier, I couldn't say it, I wanted to dance first, surprise you all.

MARTHA. You did.

BETSY. What I wanted to say was that this is my last game with the Octette Bridge Club.

LIL. What do you mean?

BETSY. Tonight is my last game.

NORA. No.

MARY. Betsy.   MARTHA. What?

ANN. Is this some kind of revenge because we didn't come to visit you?

BETSY. No, it's more than that. I get lost with all of you. I want to do my own walking

CONNIE. You've always been a walker.

BETSY. You know what I'm saying.

ALICE. Betsy, please change your mind.

LIL. Please, Betsy.

NORA. You're a part of us.

MARY. Please.

MARTHA. Don't beg. Baby brat.

BETSY. Damn it, I'm trying to grow up.

MARTHA. Stop that swearing!

BETSY. I'll speak as I please.

MARTHA. (*A volcano slowly erupts; rising.*) Oh, aren't you brave, you're so brave! Well, go, desert us! Good riddance to bad rubbish, I say.

CONNIE. That's a rotten thing to—

MARTHA. You think you're the only one who's ever suffered? Well, I know heartbreak, too, I know adultery! Michael was deserting us, leaving his family, moving out to live with a waitress, a tramp with dyed red hair. She even had the nerve to show up at his wake!

NORA. None of us knew that.

MARTHA. Do I broadcast my pain? Did I ever? No, not like some! No one knew, no one! Michael said he couldn't stand being around such a self righteous . . . prude anymore. Broke my heart . . . I know heartbreak! (*Uncontrollable sobbing takes over; pause.*) Don't anyone touch me, don't! (*pause*) I begged him to reconsider . . . got down on my knees and begged him. He agreed to stay the week. In the morning on his way to work just as he started across Main Street that drunken driver hit him. (*gaining control of herself; pause*) I don't know why I told you all that. Unless there's a lesson to be learned. Yes, yes, there is, Betsy. You see what happens to deserters? God is watching. Do you see?

BETSY. (*laughs*) I don't think I will get hit by a car tonight on my way home. If there is a God, I think he's merciful.

MARTHA. *If*? You should have your faced slapped.

BETSY. You'd be happy to do that . . . the way you did when I was a child.

MARTHA. You were only slapped if you misbehaved.

BETSY. I always misbehaved according to your—

MARTHA. You deserved it!

BETSY. You go to hell!

MARY. (*near tears*) Betsy—Martha, *stop*! (*pause*) Listen, Betsy, please. We are close. Eight of us born from the same woman, *strong* when we're together. And for me . . . it's been the joy of my life. I am so grateful for the gift of my sisters. I love you all so much. (*pause*) I won't be here much longer. There. I've said it out loud. (*pause*) Don't cry, Alice. I'm not afraid. (*pause*) Betsy, I'm not very demonstrative . . . maybe that's what you mean about us . . . come to me now. (*MARY offers her arms. BETSY doesn't move.*) Come . . . and embrace me. (*BETSY moves to her, kneels down and they embrace.*) Hug your sister, each of you. (*All hesitate, looking to one another. Then they all begin. It is slow and awkward, but an attempt. It takes time. Long pause.*)

CONNIE. (*after awkwardly hugging ANN*) You have bad breath.

ANN. I do not.

(*LIL sings a brief excerpt from a popular toothpaste jingle of the period.*)

CONNIE. We were never great huggers, any of us.

BETSY. Except me.

CONNIE. You're the exception to a lot. (*And CONNIE hugs BETSY.*)

MARY. Nice if we could live forever.

LIL. How about an old favorite? (*And she's off to the piano.*)

NORA. Good idea, Lil.

BETSY. I meant what I said.

CONNIE. I know you did. But tonight's tonight. And it's our Thirteenth Anniversary!

ALICE. Thirteen is an unlucky number.

NORA. Always was.

ANN. Always will be.

MARTHA. We're Catholics. We're not superstitious. (*They all laugh.*)

CONNIE. (*moving MARY to the piano*) Mary, before you run off into the woods with John Alden, lets sing.

(*LIL begins to play and sing an old favorite and they begin to move toward the piano, joining in the song. NORA approaches BETSY and kisses her on the cheek. Then NORA joins the singers and then BETSY does the same. But in a moment she turns around, aware of MARTHA a distance from her. She moves a step or two toward her. The two now stand on a parallel line, space between them as the singing continues and BETSY glances at MARTHA as the lights fade.*)

THE END

FURNITURE PLOT

Stage Right:
    U.R. window (with curtain & shade)
    Fireplace (mantle & fireplace set)
    D.R. window (with curtain & shade)
    Mirror above fireplace
    Wall sconces either side of fireplace
    1 Fireplace rug (small)
    Armchair D.R. — DS. of fireplace
    Magazine rack DS. of armchair D.R.
    Ottoman — in front of fireplace
    Armchair U.R. — US. of fireplace
    Floor lamp US. — of armchair U.R.

Center Upstage:
    Couch U.C.
    Credenza — U.C. above couch
    Landscape painting on wall
    Two oval family portraits on wall

Center Stage:
    2 Card tables — 1 D.L. of C.
        1 D.R. of C.
    4 Hepplewhite dining chairs —
        2 U.L. & R. of Table R.
        2 U.L. & R. of Table L.
    4 Folding wooden chairs —
        2 L. of Hepplewhites (table L. & R.)
        2 R. of Hepplewhites (table L. & R.)
    1 Persian rug

Upstage Right Wall: (Far Corner)
    Window (with curtain & shade overlooking porch)

Upstage Left Wall: (Far Corner)
What-not shelf with china objects on wall.

Stage Left:
Piano — against s.l. wall
Piano stool — c. of piano
Small piano rug
Window (curtain & shade) us. of piano
1 Radiator us. of piano
Floor lamp us. of piano
Seascape painting on wall above piano
Armchair dl. — ds. of piano
Small end table — behind dl. armchair
Small quarter moon size and shape end table
   against ds. arm of dl. armchair

Stage Right Foyer:
Sliding doors (or archway) into living room
Door to outside
Closet door (partially visible)
Mirror on wall us. of front door
Small end table below mirror
1 Small hallway rug
1 Chandelier
Staircase (optional)

Stage Left Dining Room:
Sliding glass doors (or archway) into dining room
Door us. to kitchen
1 pair sheer curtains on dining room doors
Dining room table (partially visible)
2 Hepplewhite arm dining chairs
Window sl. wall (curtain and shade)
1 Rug
1 Chandelier

PROPERTY LIST

ACT ONE, Scene 1

PRESET:

Mantle:
2 Vases with pussywillows
5 Family photos
1 Candy dish (with candy)
1 purse (Connie)

Magazine Rack
1934 Magazines

s.l. Armchair u.r.
1 purse (Nora)

Credenza
1 Table lamp
1 Candy dish (with candy)
2 Card boxes (space for 2 decks of cards)
2 Score pads with pencils
1 Purse (Betsy)

Card Tables
1 Deck of cards at each table

Couch
2 Pillows
3 Purses (Mary, Alice, Lil)

Piano
Sheet music on piano face
Atop Piano:
Pile of sheet music
Piano lamp

2 Small jack-o-lanterns (with candy)
1 Purse (Martha)

Dining Room Table
 1 Plate of cookies
 Napkins

Antimacassars
 4 3 piece sets on armchairs and couch

Camera with Flash Attachment on Tripod (D.L.)
 1 Camera box (with flash bulbs) in front of D.L.
 armchair

Offstage Left: (Kitchen)
 1 Glass of ginger ale (Lil)
 1 Glass of water (Ann)
 1 Glass of ginger ale (Ann)

In Unseen Closet:
 Coat and hat (Martha)
 Coat and hat (Mary)
 Coat and hat (Nora)
 Coat and hat (Connie)
 Coat and hat (Alice)
 Coat and hat (Lil)
 Coat and hat (Betsy)
 Shawl or sweater (Ann)

Personal Props:
 Set of car and house keys (Connie)
 Reporter's notebook and pencil (Foster)
 Small pillbox (Mary)

ACT ONE Scene 2*

PRESET:

1 Glass of ginger ale (Martha)
1 Cup and saucer (Mary)
1 Cup and saucer (Connie)
1 Plate of half finished cake on piano (Lil)
1 Napkin (on couch)

ACT TWO

PRESET:

Living Room: (Replacements and Additions)
  Venetian blinds (replacing window shades)
  Piano bench (replacing piano stool)
  4 Sets of opaque curtains on windows
  4 Valance boxes
  3 new 1940 lampshades
  1 Slipcover for couch and matching upholstered seat cushions
  1 Slipcover for D.R. armchair and matching upholstered cushion
  1 Slipcover for U.R. armchair and matching upholstered cushion
  1 Throw for DL. armchair
  1 Large photo of the Octette Bridge Club, 1934 (replacing landscape center wall)
  1 "Boy in service" banner for UR. window
  1940's sheet music

---

*NOTE: Quilted table tops and fake table tops can be used on card tables for quick changes between the scenes.

1 Console radio (floor model)
1 Wheelchair (Mary)
1 Basket attached to wheelchair
1 Cane (Martha)
2 Nut dishes (1 on mantle, 1 on credenza)
3 Family photos added to mantle
2 Vases now contain autumn leaves

Also on Mantle:

1 Pottery container with 8 slips of paper and 8 pencils
2 Empty card boxes

Card Tables:

2 Decks of cards (2 at each table)
Pencils
Scoring pads (with names written in)
1 Rack for holding hand of cards (Mary)
2 glasses of water with straws (for Mary)
And the 7 ladies' purses (optional)

Dining Room:

1 Plate of cookies
1 Red parasol (Lil)
1 Small wicker basket with arm handle (Lil)
1 Glass "boat shaped" container with green bath oil beads wrapped in wrapping paper with ribbons (Ann)

Offstage in Closet:

John the Baptist papier mache head on tray (Betsy)

ACT TWO, Scene 2

PRESET:

1 Glass of ginger ale (Martha)
1 Dessert plate with fake crumbs and fork attached
2 Potlids (Ann)

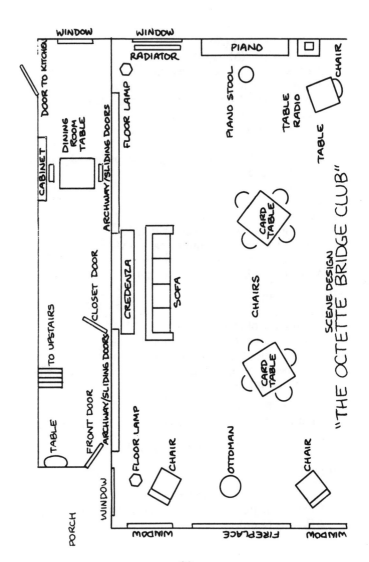

SCENE DESIGN
"THE OCTETTE BRIDGE CLUB"

90

Other Publications for Your Interest

NOISES OFF
(LITTLE THEATRE—FARCE)

By MICHAEL FRAYN

5 men, 4 women—2 Interiors

This wonderful Broadway smash hit is "a farce about farce, taking the clichés of the genre and shaking them inventively through a series of kaleidoscopic patterns. Never missing a trick, it has as its first act a pastiche of traditional farce; as its second, a contemporary variant on the formula; as its third, an elaborate undermining of it. The play opens with a touring company dress-rehearsing 'Nothing On', a conventional farce. Mixing mockery and homage, Frayn heaps into this play-within-a-play a hilarious melee of stock characters and situations. Caricatures—cheery char, outraged wife and squeaky blonde—stampede in and out of doors. Voices rise and trousers fall . . . a farce that makes you think as well as laugh."—London Times Literary Supplement. ". . . as side-splitting a farce as I have seen. Ever? *Ever.*"—John Simon, NY Magazine. "The term 'hilarious' must have been coined in the expectation that something on the order of this farce-within-a-farce would eventually come along to justify it."—N.Y. Daily News. "Pure fun."—N.Y. Post. "A joyous and loving reminder that the theatre really does go on, even when the show falls apart."—N.Y. Times.   (#16052)

THE REAL THING
(ADVANCED GROUPS—COMEDY)

By TOM STOPPARD

4 men, 3 women—Various settings

The effervescent Mr. Stoppard has never been more intellectually—and *emotionally*—engaging than in this "backstage" comedy about a famous playwright named Henry Boot whose second wife, played on Broadway to great acclaim by Glenn Close (who won the Tony Award), is trying to merge "worthy causes" (generally a euphemism for left-wing politics) with her art as an actress. She has met a "political prisoner" named Brodie who has been jailed for radical thuggery, and who has written an inept play about how property is theft, about how the State stifles the Rights of The Individual, etc., etc., etc. Henry's wife wants him to make the play work theatrically, which he does after much soul-searching. Eventually, though, he is able to convince his wife that Brodie is emphatically *not* a victim of political repression. He is, in fact, a thug. Famed British actor Jeremy Irons triumphed in the Broadway production (Tony Award), which was directed to perfection by none other than Mike Nichols (Tony Award). "So densely and entertainingly packed with wit, ideas and feelings that one visit just won't do . . . Tom Stoppard's most moving play and the most bracing play anyone has written about love and marriage in years."—N.Y. Times. "Shimmering, dazzling theatre, a play of uncommon wit and intelligence which not only thoroughly delights but challenges and illuminates our lives."—WCBS-TV. 1984 Tony Award-Best Play.   (#941)

COUNT DRACULA

TED TILLER

(All Groups) Mystery comedy

7 Men, 2 Women. Interior with Small Inset

1930 Costumes (optional)

Based on Bram Stoker's 19th Century novel, "Dracula." This is a new, witty version of the classic story of a suave vampire whose passion is sinking his teeth into the throats of beautiful young women. Mina, his latest victim, is the ward of Dr. Seward in whose provincial insane asylum the terrifying action transpires. Her finance arrives from London, worried over her strange inertia and trance-like state. Equally concerned is Professor Van Helsing, specialist in rare maladies, who senses the supernatural at work. Added trouble comes from Sybil, Dr. Sewards demented, sherry-tippling sister and from Renfield, a schizophrenic inmate in league with the vampire. But how to trap this ghoul who can transform himself into a bat, materialize from fog, dissolve in mist? There are many surprising but uncomplicated stage effects, mysterious disappearances, secret panels, howling wolves, bats that fly over the audience, an unexpected murder, and magic tricks which include Dracula's vanishing in full view of the spectators.

> Despite much gore, ". . . the play abounds with funny lines. There is nothing in it but entertainment."—*Springfield, Mass. News.*

FRANKENSTEIN

TIM KELLY

(All Groups)

4 Men, 4 Women, Interior

Victor Frankenstein, a brilliant young scientist, returns to his chateau on the shores of Lake Geneva to escape some terrible pursuer. No one can shake free the dark secret that terrifies him. Not his mother, nor his financee Elizabeth, nor his best friend, Henry Clerval. Even the pleading of a gypsy girl accused of murdering Victor's younger brother falls on deaf ears, for Victor has brought into being a "Creature" made from bits and pieces of the dead! The Creature tracks Victor to his sanctuary to demand a bride to share its loneliness—one as wretched as the Creature itself. Against his better judgment, Victor agrees and soon the household is invaded by murder, despair and terror! The play opens on the wedding night of Victor and Elizabeth, the very time the Creature has sworn to kill the scientist for destroying its intended mate, and ends, weeks later, in a horrific climax of dramatic suspense! In between there is enough macabre humor to relieve the mounting tension. Perhaps the truest adaptation of Mary Shelley's classic yet. Simple to stage and a guaranteed audience pleaser.

Other Publications for Your Interest

A WEEKEND NEAR MADISON
(LITTLE THEATRE—COMIC DRAMA)
By KATHLEEN TOLAN

2 men, 3 women—Interior

This recent hit from the famed Actors Theatre of Louisville, a terrific ensemble play about male-female relationships in the 80's, was praised by *Newsweek* as "warm, vital, glowing . . . full of wise ironies and unsentimental hopes". The story concerns a weekend reunion of old college friends now in their early thirties. The occasion is the visit of Vanessa, the queen bee of the group, who is now the leader of a lesbian/feminist rock band. Vanessa arrives at the home of an old friend who is now a psychiatrist hand in hand with her naif-like lover, who also plays in the band. Also on hand are the psychiatrist's wife, a novelist suffering from writer's block; and his brother, who was once Vanessa's lover and who still loves her. In the course of the weekend, Vanessa reveals that she and her lover desperately want to have a child—and she tries to persuade her former male lover to father it, not understanding that he might have some feelings about the whole thing. *Time Magazine* heard "the unmistakable cry of an infant hit . . . Playwright Tolan's work radiates promise and achievement."   (#25051)

PASTORALE
(LITTLE THEATRE—COMEDY)
By DEBORAH EISENBERG

3 men, 4 women—Interior
(plus 1 or 2 bit parts and 3 optional extras)

"Deborah Eisenberg is one of the freshest and funniest voices in some seasons."—Newsweek. Somewhere out in the country Melanie has rented a house and in the living room she, her friend Rachel who came for a weekend but forgets to leave, and their school friend Steve (all in their mid-20s) spend nearly a year meandering through a mental landscape including such concerns as phobias, friendship, work, sex, slovenliness and epistemology. Other people happen by: Steve's young girlfriend Celia, the virtuous and annoying Edie, a man who Melanie has picked up in a bar, and a couple who appear during an intense conversation and observe the sofa is on fire. The lives of the three friends inevitably proceed and eventually draw them, the better prepared perhaps by their months on the sofa, in separate directions. "The most original, funniest new comic voice to be heard in New York theater since Beth Henley's 'Crimes of the Heart.'"—N.Y. Times. "A very funny, stylish comedy."—The New Yorker. "Wacky charm and wayward wit."—New York Magazine. "Delightful."—N.Y. Post. "Uproarious . . . the play is a world unto itself, and it spins."—N.Y. Sunday Times.   (#18016)

Other Publications for Your Interest

HUSBANDRY
(LITTLE THEATRE—DRAMA)

By PATRICK TOVATT

2 men, 2 women—Interior

At its recent world premiere at the famed Actors Theatre of Louisville, this enticing new drama moved an audience of theatre professionals up off their seats and on to their feet to cheer. Mr. Tovatt has given us an insightful drama about what is happening to the small, family farm in America—and what this means for the future of the country. The scene is a farmhouse whose owners are on the verge of losing their farm. They are visited by their son and his wife, who live "only" eight hours' drive away. The son has a good job in the city, and his wife does, too. The son, Harry, is really put on the horns of a dilemma when he realizes that he is his folks' only hope. The old man can't go it alone anymore—and he needs his son. Pulling at him from the other side is his wife, who does not want to leave her job and uproot her family to become a farm wife. *Husbandry*, then, is ultimately about what it means to be a *husband*—both in the farm and in the family sense. *Variety* praised the "delicacy of Tovatt's dialogue", and called the play "a literate exploration of family responsibilities in a mobile society." Said *Time*: "The play simmers so gently for so long, as each potential confrontation is deflected with Chekhovian shrugs and silences, that when it boils into hostility it sears the audience." (#10169)

CLARA'S PLAY
(LITTLE THEATRE—DRAMA)

By JOHN OLIVE

3 men, 1 woman—Exterior

Clara, an aging spinster, lives alone in a remote farmhouse. She is the last surviving member of one of the area's most prominent families. It is summer, 1915. Enter an immigrant, feisty soul named Sverre looking for a few days' work before moving on. But Clara's farm needs more than just a few days' work, and Sverre stays on to help Clara fix up and run the farm. It soon becomes clear unscrupulous local businessmen are bilking Clara out of money and hope to gain control of her property. Sverre agrees to stay on to help Clara keep her family's property. "A story of determination, loyalty. It has more than a measure of love, of resignation, of humor and loyalty."—Chicago Sun-Times. "A playwright of unusual sensitivity in delineating character and exploring human relationships." —Chicago Tribune. "Gracefully-written, with a real sense of place."—Village Voice. A recent success both at Chicago's fine Wisdom Bridge Theatre and at the Great American Play Festival of the world-reknowned Actors Theatre of Louisville; and, on tour, starring Jean Stapleton. (#5076)